AFRICAN AMERICAN HERBALISM & MAGICK

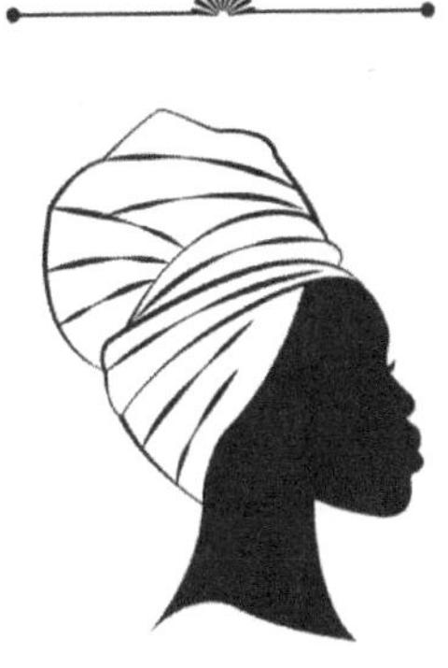

AFRICAN AMERICAN HERBALISM & MAGICK

CLICK HERE

Or Visit Below:

https://www.subscribepage.com/svmyth

Simply scan the qr code to join.

CONTENTS

INTRODUCTION 1

CHAPTER 1: THE LEGACY OF AFRICAN AMERICAN HERBALISTS AND MAGICK PRACTIONERS 14

DOCTOR CAESAR 16
EMMA DUPREE 17
HENRIETTA PHELPS JEFFERIES 19
DR. SEBI 20
EMPRESS KAREN ROSE 24

CHAPTER 2: UNDERSTANDING THE BASICS OF HERBAL MAGICK 30

CHAPTER 3: SACRED PLANTS AND HOLISTIC USE 44

MAYPOP 47
MUGWORT 53
SASSAFRAS 56
CONEFLOWER 59
GOLDENSEAL 62
HOREHOUND 64
A POWER THAT SPANS GENERATIONS 66

CHAPTER 4: THE ART OF ANCESTRAL COMMUNICATION AND DIVINATION 70

WHAT IS ANCESTRAL COMMUNICATION AND DIVINATION?
.... 71
IMPORTANT SPIRITUAL SIGNIFICANCE 74
TRADITIONAL METHODS EXPLAINED 75
ETHICAL RESPONSIBILITY 84

CHAPTER 5: IN THE SPIRIT OF COMMUNITY

AND HEALING **88**

THE ROLE OF COMMUNITY IN HEALING 90
COMMUNAL HEALING THROUGH HERBALISM 91
MAGICK AND COLLECTIVE TRANSFORMATION 93
CULTIVATING RESILIENCE AND BELONGING 101

CHAPTER 6: TRADITIONAL HERBAL REMEDIES **106**

THE WISDOM OF ANCESTRAL HERBALISM..................108
HERBAL TEA NOURISHMENT 109
POTENT HERBAL TINCTURES 114
CRAFTING PROTECTION WITH HERBAL SALVES.......... 120

CHAPTER 7: PURIFYING THE BODY, MIND, AND SPIRIT THROUGH SPIRITUAL BATHS AND CLEANSING RITUALS **126**

ORIGINS OF SPIRITUAL BATHS AND CLEANSING RITUALS
.... 128
SIGNIFICANCE OF SPIRITUAL BATHS AND CLEANSING
RITUALS IN AFRICAN AMERICAN HERBALISM 130
PREPARING FOR SPIRITUAL BATHS OR CLEANSING
RITUALS...131
CREATING THE SACRED BATH 133
CONDUCTING THE CLEANSING RITUAL....................... 134

CHAPTER 8: ANCESTRAL RITUALS AND BEHAVIORS **140**

ANCIENT RITUAL HISTORY AND TRADITION 141
RITUAL BEHAVIORS AND OBSERVANCES...................... 147
HEALING BATH RITUALS 150
PROTECTION WITH SACRED STONES OR CRYSTALS 157
PROSPERITY RITUAL WITH HERBAL SACHETS 159

CHAPTER 9: COMMUNITY AND HEALING ...166

Historical Context and the Roots of Herbalism
and Magick 168
Herbalism in the African American Community . 170
Magick and Spirituality 172
Healing From Collective Trauma 175
A Sense of Belonging in Resistance 179

CHAPTER 10: LOOKING FORWARD............. 190

Challenges Facing African American Herbalism
and Magick 192
Opportunities for Growth..................................... 194
The Evolving Landscape of Spiritual Practice... 198

REFERENCES 201

INTRODUCTION

The realm of African American herbalism and magick is rich with cultural heritage and historical significance. However, it has often been overshadowed by misconceptions and false information, largely due to historical biases. Some misconceptions give reference to magickal practices as being evil, with spells, potions, and incantations fueled with blood sacrifice. These misconceptions persist despite the availability of vast amounts of information in the modern age, making it crucial to address and correct them. People seeking authentic knowledge are found overwhelmed with resources, such as blogs and lifestyle websites; however, they provide inaccuracies of cultural practices.

One primary reason for the proliferation of false information surrounding African

American herbalism and magick is the historical marginalization and suppression of African knowledge systems during periods of slavery and colonialism. As tribal people were forcibly displaced from their homelands and subjected to cultural erasure, their traditional practices and healing rituals were often demonized or dismissed as primitive superstition. This resulted in a distortion of understanding and a perpetuation of stereotypes that influence perceptions.

In the digital age, where information spreads quickly via online platforms and social media, the likelihood of encountering misinformation is high. Technology provides a platform for inaccurate and culturally insensitive information.

Authentic Connection to Ancestral Wisdom

Individuals seeking to reconnect with ancestral roots are likely in search of deeper self-understanding. Embarking on a journey to consciously embrace traditional African American practices is like breathing life into the intentions of the ancestors, all the while setting foot towards reconnecting to the roots of tradition and the holistic use of plant life. The power in this lies within the knowledge of cultural foundation and ancient wisdom. Historical context serves as a reminder that amidst adversity, resilience mixed with the many wonders of herbalism through spirituality remains to be effective armor for the African American suit of life. Spirituality was such an essential part of ancestral herbalism and was used to fortify as well as bring healing within the community. Profound insight can come from ancient wisdoms. However, most humans do not understand that the harmony one seeks is subjective. Applying these practices to modern-day life is meant to be individualistic and empowering. Resonating powerfully in cultural rediscovery is the triumph of the ancestors.

Holistic Health Approach

Ancient traditions allocate healing plants, oils, teas, and tinctures for holistic health practices. Living in a world where pharmaceuticals rule the medical paradigm, individuals now eagerly seek alternatives to better health. Conventional medicine falls short of spiritual nourishment as it is neglected in the pharmaceutical-driven healthcare approach. People are frustrated with life imbalances and are developing a new appreciation for mental, spiritual, and emotional wellness. The literary market feeds this newfound awareness with a surge of comprehensive guides positioning themselves as beacons of hope to a life of vitality. Frustration with the health administration is a guiding force behind finding new avenues to physical and spiritual balance. These books are comprehensive roadmaps for those pivoting to a holistic lifestyle.

Natural and Spiritual Healing

Increased interest in the spiritual dimensions of healing has led to an increased number of natural or herbal medicine practitioners. What was once considered a taboo art has now become a mainstream lifestyle. It is now a dinner table conversation or one of the causal reads in your  carry-on luggage. A growing curiosity toward the subject matter has birthed a plethora of books offering practical guidelines for holistic healing modalities. These books are invaluable resources for those eager to transform, practice, or simply become more knowledgeable about alternative medicine.

Searching for Healing Amidst Trauma

Being in search of something new and enriching empowers the individual to heal from traumas. As many continue to grapple with the horrific truths of slavery and its generational effects, books delving into the thick of African American ancestral spirituality provide tools for healing. The challenges of ongoing racial injustices and the general breathing while melanated have led many to find solace in the wisdom of ancestral traditions. Steering the seas of deeper meaning to strengthen holistic self-care while cultivating a deep healing connection with Earth's sacred flora is a mission supported through ongoing research.

To Learn and Practice Safely

There must be a desire for readers to learn, and for some, an inevitable need to practice spirituality. Take into account that aspiring practitioners of herbalism and magick are guided to use integrity with respect to ancient teachings. To engage in these necessary sacred practices, guidance is needed to effectively connect with the spirits and the natural world. Even if traditions are passed down, written reference is an essential resource. Comprehensive guides emphasizing hands-on learning with creative influences and insightful interpretation of the healing powers of plants provide indoctrination for the retention of teachings.

Combating Misinformation

Honoring the sapience of the past in an era of misinformation is critical for the new practitioners of African American traditions. Books combatting falsehoods of the heritage with well-researched content serve as preservers of truth. In the realm of African American magick, accurately delineating the rich tapestry of cultural wonder disarms apprehension of the unknown. Meticulous attention to detail with a commitment to historical accuracy dismantles misconceptions. This offers the reader a chance to build perception through the integrity of authentic knowledge. A chance to deconstruct stereotypes with informative empathy.

Reconnecting With Ancestral Wisdom

Appreciation amongst readers from all walks of life lends to the demand for practical guides with explanatory details to spiritual practices. The masses deem that the times call for a reconnection to ancestral wisdom and these books provide narratives emphasizing the historical significance of various practices. They help readers to appreciate their roots and grasp a better understanding of what it meant for the ancestors to be resilient. Tales of historical figures illuminate culture with invaluable advice. Vivid references contextualizing rituals and beliefs paint the frameworks of legacy. These narratives give the reader individualized pathways to incorporate these traditions into their personal lives. Encouraging them to reclaim regency in their cultural identity by bridging the gap between past and present. Seeking this type of knowledge is like bringing life to the voices of the past, fostering connection while honoring one's heritage.

Promoting Holistic Health

Books offering holistic teachings about the integration of physical, spiritual, and emotional wellness are indispensable to those who seek balance. Acting as not just a guide providing practical application of the use of herbs for diet and rituals, they also act as a manual supporting interconnectedness of the mind, body, and spirit. The pro-holistic health approach substantiates how the inner workings of modern science and ancient wisdom create a unique space for the individual to discover a deeper understanding of self. Assiduous delivery of recipes to sustain health or remedy illness and conscious nourishment feeds the idea of optimum health. Individuals find these resources to provide a wealth of information to serve as tools steering them along in their personal journeys to prosperity with intention.

Facilitating Natural and Spiritual Healing

Utilizing a holistic approach to thrive in all levels of lifefacilitates natural and spiritual healing. Using these resources as the guiding light for technique into self-healing is all a part of acknowledging the significance of ancestral practices. Tools of empowerment made into step-by-step guides ignite transformative action to live authentically. Honoring the wisdom of spirit with knowledge satiates the subconscious mind of the reader. Readers kindle a cognizance that aligns with the rhythmic gifts of nature that is inclusive of conducting rituals and engaging in these practices.

Empowering Readers Amidst Trauma

Functioning as powerful vessels of empowerment amidst trauma, readers are offered a beacon of enlightenment. As we know, with knowledge comes power and some would even say great responsibility. This enlightenment fortifies the mindset necessary for the journey. It carries the message of triumph through generations of oppression. Through storytelling, readers are invited into a communal space of healing by understanding the practices of ancestral lineage as well as the strength and courage drawn from the resilience of a people. Readers find a sense of belonging and identity to forge purposeful pathways towards healing.

Ensuring Safe Practice and Learning

Resources provide practical advice that allows the reader to safely commence their journey with ethics and respect for preservation. Prioritizing detailed guidelines of herbal usage and other considerable practices shows mindful reverence to the heritage. Foregrounding principles of reciprocity, readers are able to gradually incorporate herbalism and African American spiritual rituals into daily life. Whether harvesting mindfulness of the medicinal wonders of plants or engaging African

American traditions in a fashion promoting cultural preservation, rich historical context lends to personal growth and collective healing.

Educating on Authentic Practices

Benefits are abundant and found in appreciation of the unique blend of cultural heritage, ancestral wisdom, and insightful holistic health. These types of resources cater to the correction of misinformation by shedding misconceptions through researched truths of African American traditions. They position themselves as the ropes on the bridge to a deeper ancestral connection, allowing readers to become better acquainted with their roots with esteem to the contribution of African American herbalists throughout history.

Now that the tone has been set, let's dive into  the transformative world of *African American Herbalism and Magick.* A world filled with the secrets of herbalists of generations past. Offering more than just knowledge, this book compels a profound understanding of holistic healing, practical herbal wisdom, dynamic cultural connection, and the powerful integration of magick into everyday life. Facts have been verified by experts and attested by countless reader testimonials. There is a dire need for authenticity, spiritual empowerment, and holistic healing in a world seemingly charged with superficial complacency. Acquiring this book means you will partake in the movement of grounded self-fulfillment by acknowledging that health is wealth and wealth is a more spiritually enriched life. Integrating magickal practices into your routine is embracing ancestral wisdom. Readers must be open to a metamorphic journey of wellness through a deeper connection to the natural and spirit world.

CHAPTER 1
THE LEGACY OF AFRICAN AMERICAN HERBALISTS AND MAGICK PRACTIONERS

To appreciate the gifts of African American herbalism, we must first take notice of its significance in the Western World. Let's unwrap the essence of magick while taking time to appreciate those who keep the ancient wisdom alive. It is important to understand that people once took to these types of healing practices by way of survival. Spirituality and holistic medicine of the African American culture are rooted in resilience through adversity. History holsters the experiences of those who contributed significantly to the evolution of these practices. With lore and ritual passed down through generations, the legacy lies within cultural knowledge. This chapter will explore several key figures such as Dr. Sebi, Emma Dupree, Doctor Caesar, Karen Rose, and Henrietta Phelps Jeffries. It will shed light on how they dedicated their lives to carry on ancestral legacy, both in the traditional and modern context.

There was a time when practice of African American spirituality was banned and the rituals of magick seen as treacherously taboo. In turn slave communities found solace in the secrecy of ancestral traditions. Forbidden from basic reading and writing, oral history was of grave importance for survival. Often overlooked, the legacies of practitioners have shaped modern-day practice.

Doctor Caesar

Masters of African American herbalism use plant-based concoctions with the control of herb interactions to assist the community. A rooted example is Doctor Caesar, an enslaved man and medical practitioner, who was the first African American to have his medical findings printed in the media. His actual name is unknown, much like the significance of his connection to the herbs. What we do know is that before law was issued preventing enslaved healers from aiding others who were enslaved medically, Doctor Caesar cured people of suspected poisoning. Acknowledged for having cured several people, this life-saving antidote was made by grinding the roots of plantain (narrowleaf) and horehound, boiling the herbs with quarts of water 2:1, then straining it for consumption on an empty stomach.

He also is historically known to have presented the cure for rattlesnake bites and a variety of other ailments. By taking the same herbs (narrowleaf and horehound) and bruising them in a mortar, you have prepared the basic elements for rattlesnake bite relief. The liquid must be squeezed out to be taken orally, one tablespoon at a time.

It was said that the herbal blend generally worked after the first dose. However, the healer could administer a second dose if there was no relief after the first hour.

Through his medical findings, Doctor Caesar was granted his freedom in 1750, sometime in his late 60s. It was said that he passed away around March of 1754. His short but sweet taste of freedom is an authentic example of the ways African American ancestral healing techniques help one to endure the challenges of life.

Emma Dupree

A gem in her time, we give reverence to the lovely Emma Dupree. From the age of six, she understood that she had a special relationship with plant life. The daughter of freed North Carolina slaves, Emma embraced the responsibility of the connection by sharing her holistic remedies and meals. She became known as "Little Medicine Thing" while working beside her husband at his job in the local doctor's office. Learning a lot from the doctors, she was able to identify and manipulate the benefits of the herbs she helped to stock. Eventually upon the occasional incurable disease or unidentifiable condition as determined by a doctor, patients often sought Mrs. Dupree's holistic guidance. Her healing gifts expanded beyond the physical realm as she proclaimed that there was always spiritual intention guiding her efforts. *"Take this medicine with faith. I am just the instrument"* (Dupree, n.d). The effects of her medicine were

appreciated for working just as well as prescription, if not better. Burning bush to decoct herbal essence became a smell that kept a line to her backyard. People often mentioned the healing effects in the warmth of her conversation.

Taking pride in her garden and the wonders the Earth provides, Emma Dupree was a self-proclaimed herbalist from childhood. She spent her adult life treating pneumonia, influenza, diabetes, and many other ailments without the manmade boundaries of color. She was a beacon of herbal wisdom and an advocate for holistic wellness. She believed that wellness was more than fighting the occasional illness or combating old age. It was the way we consume our food, from the type of heat used to the device used to conduct the heat, all of which she believed altered the effects of digested food. She treated fever with horseradish leaves, Epsom salt, and vinegar. She used wild cherries, honey, and rock candy as blood toner. Sage to pull the bacteria from pork while cooking it to temperature or steeping the bark of a maypop tree for a delicious anti-inflammatory tea (also serving equally as potent to decrease anxiety and insomnia). Leaving this realm in the year of 1996 at the age of 82, her commitment to natural remedy resonates in her lifelong efforts to empower the community with holistic wellness practices.

Henrietta Phelps Jefferies

One of the more infamously known contributors to African American magick and herbalism is Henrietta Phelps Jefferies, who was also known as Aunt Henrietta. Henrietta was a Virginia midwife born a slave but later emancipated. She was married at 15, then widowed and remarried at 23. A mother of 18 children, by the age of 54 Henrietta found herself in defense of her services as a midwife to many. Charged with practicing medicine without a license on the wives of slave owners, she was ultimately shown empathy by the judge. However, it was ordered for her to not treat any other birthing mothers with natural remedies or herbal medicine besides turpentine and tansy tea. Henrietta was recognized as an herbal woman or what they called an "old granny lady" back then. The judge couldn't deny her freedom as he was one of twelve siblings brought into this world by Henrietta.

It is important to note the resistance of slave owners and their professional counterparts in African American herbal healing practices. Known as slave medicine, herbal healing practices were mostly suppressed. Being removed from their homeland and stripped from traditional African ritual, slaves used the influences of the Native Americans in conjunction with European immigrants to gather generations worth of natural medicinal knowledge. Holistic healing was often seen as more effective than medicine given by medical counterparts of slave owners. It is the careful manipulation of herbs by slaves that lend to the many plant-based remedies we use today.

Dr. Sebi

Dr. Sebi, born Alfredo Bowman, is a controversial figure in the legacy of African American herbalism. As he was Honduran, Dr.

Sebi's work has proven to transcend the research of his American ancestors. At a time in his youth when he was diagnosed with asthma, diabetes, impotence, and obesity, Dr. Sebi found a cure for all in the ancient powers of herbs. He was treated of his ailments in Mexico by a man who practiced magick through herbal medicine, Alfredo Cortez, he was encouraged to seek longevity in the holistic wisdom of his roots. As a genetically African man, the herbalist advised him to follow an original African diet.

Though inspired by the treatment of his own illnesses, Dr. Sebi attributes his love for the natural to his grandmother. He did not attend formal school, but with the pillars of his foundation and a fascination for what the earth naturally provides, a world-renowned natural doctor to the people was born. His lifelong interest in plants was a catalyst for his ambitions to treat chronic illness with herbal food remedies. Remedies were based on the philosophy of an alkaline plant-based diet. It was his second wife that gave him the name Sebi. The locals called him "doctor" after proven success with his experiments on members of the community. A prosperous life with 22 children and four wives certainly validates that he was healed of impotence.

A prime example of reversing poor health through the power of herbs, Sebi used his discoveries to further develop his healing practices for the use of the masses. He expanded his scope of practice to the U.S. while still keeping a presence in Honduras. He was sought after by famous celebrities and high-profile people seeking alternative remedies to what the doctors may prescribe. Claims of him curing AIDS, cancer, and a wide range of other ailments led to the development of a special treatment therapy called, African Bio-Electric Cell Food Therapy. Described as a health management system that restores the body to its natural alkaline state.

Dr. Sebi's formula for optimum health was a combination of plant-based science and alkaline daily nutrition with the belief that it is just as important to identify the cause of the illness as it is to treat it. By finding that the cause of disease is mucus, his methodology was to use naturally alkaline plant life to detoxify the body while replenishing it with vital minerals at the same time. His nutritional guidelines worked so well that news of its dramatic effects circulated quickly. Word of life-changing effects from restoring the body to peak health reached the ears of Michael Jackson, John Travolta, Lisa "Left Eye" Lopes, Teddy Pendergrass, Erykah Badu, and even Eddie Murphy. Ultimately reaching millions through testimony alone.

Controversy ensued in the form of arrests and lawsuits against Sebi. In 1988, New York State filed the first lawsuit making claims that he was practicing medicine without a license. He was acquitted by defense of not practicing allopathic Western medicine. The second lawsuit ordered Sebi to stop the claims that any of his remedies cured serious illness a few years later. This pushed him to Los Angeles where he acquired his celebrity clientele. There is controversy surrounding his death in 2016. It's said that his death was a conspiracy carried out because of his threat to the pharmaceutical industry. Despite said controversy, Dr. Sebi is seen as a true healer of his people and was widely known to advocate self-love and spiritual health awareness. His legacy lives on in USHA Village, a tropical retreat in Honduras meant for transformative healing of the body using his African Bio-Mineral Therapy Program.

Empress Karen Rose

A Master Herbalist of today known as Empress Karen Rose, captured the knowledge given to her from her Guyanese grandmother to the streets of Brooklyn. She is formally trained in both Western and Eastern herbal medicine with a strong  appreciation for ancestral herbalism. Rose openly acknowledges that it is vital to plant medicine to understand the herbs of the land we inhabit. Growing up in the coastal Amazon gave Rose exposure to Latin American, Caribbean, and African herbalism. With this influence, she was driven to community healing with the mission to remind people of the connectivity to spirit and plant life.

Dedicated to community healing Rose opened Sacred Vibes Healing and Sacred Vibes Apothecary in 2002. Her mission to reconnect the African American diaspora to the power of herbs is fulfilled daily within the walls of her apothecaries. Alongside her extensive line of herbal products, Empress Karen Rose offers an herbalism apprenticeship and mentorship program. Since 2018 she has hosted the Annual Black Herbalist Convergence where those in attendance gather to absorb the wisdom of Rose and other platform healers. It is an event meant to connect people to accessible healers, serving as a safe place for the African American community to reclaim their heritage through reconnection of spirit in the roots of ancestral herbalism.

As life flows through the river of time, Rose's wisdom has become more expansive as an astrologer, author, and medicine woman. She later opened a consultation space known as Sacred Botanica. A space where the powers of herbal magick bridge diverse communities who are deprived of spiritual healing or lack the knowledge thereof. With the emphasis that spiritual healing is the path to self-truths, her platform encompasses ritual that nourishes mind, body, and soul. Her teachings are meant to remind us that healing of the physical is one and the same as emotional and spiritual. Her newest space is an extension of the magick in her physical services offering consultation, spiritual assistance, and tarot readings. Empress Karen Rose has been featured in a variety of media outlets including the New York Times. She has written a number of articles regarding her teachings and is even featured alongside celebrity Chef Marcus Samuelsson in The FEED.

The bequest of African American herbalism with the art of magick is full of colorful patches of experiences. It is a fact that we are now living in times where one is constitutionally free to practice their beliefs without harm to others. However, many still find the traditional rituals of the African diaspora as dark magic or spell work and the other variations. Figures like Dr. Sebi and Empress Karen Rose are relied upon for guidance and reassurance in the evidence that magick through plant medicine can be effective. They give new practitioners of magick and herbalism inspiration to continue their strides in enriching the community to wellness naturally.

Unbeknownst to the practitioners of the past is the historical testament to how tradition transcends time. Pioneering work in holistic healing, Doctor Caesar will have an eternal imprint in the medical world. Henrietta's gifts live within the children she brought into this realm safely as well as the mothers she helped to bring forth life. She lives even in the depths of the lives of their offspring. Although still often overlooked and marginalized, the African American people can feed from these contributions to enhance their lifestyle through understanding of the ancestors and their resourceful resilience.

CHAPTER 2
UNDERSTANDING THE BASICS OF HERBAL MAGICK

When we think about herbal magick we must consider the ancient tapestry of human history; of how we are adaptive, resourceful creatures with interwoven threads of ancestral wisdoms. Our differences in experiences are what create unique patterns in the ripples of time. They are what sets the scene for folklore while consequently creating the basis for misinformed stereotypes. From genesis, civilization has sought the potency of power within the natural arts harnessed through Earth's gift of plant life.

Not to confuse smoke and mirrors with the vibrating energies of intention, magick can be seen as a form of spiritual enlightenment. A little known mental practice that consciously harnesses the strength in the elements and is deeply rooted in the knowledge of herbal ritual. Practitioners are met with a major responsibility to honor the mystical connection of plants and consciousness. In this chapter, we'll take a little time to build some structure around the foundation of the ancestors by gaining some basic understanding of the practice of herbal magick.

Take the time to uncover how energy, intention, and the consciousness of plant life are fundamental to understanding the principles of practice. These properties are what steer the ship of holistic healing in the uneasy waters of adversity, allowing spiritual enlightenment to grant them light in this sometimes dark world. With the divine light of natural philosophy, practitioners are naturally inclined to spiritual intervention. They must rely on the succession of ancestral conceptions, and the integrity of ritual. What the masses can't seem to acknowledge is the mindfulness behind the practice.

Herbal magick centralizes the power of intention, which in turn transfers energy directly from the intention of the practitioner into meaningful work or services. Herbal medicine serves the purpose of healing physical ailments, though also serving as a powerful stimulus for spiritual wellness. Spiritual beings who seek comprehension of the depths of the natural world find solace in the honor of keeping its secrets. The practicing collective has to organically trust in the spirit of nature and sensibly partner with the elements. The healing ritual must be imbued with the intention to work effectively. This belief is grounded in the interconnectedness of all that inhabits the universe. It is an understanding that the unique vibrations of plant life possess certain properties that harness magickal frequencies. Encompassing a wide range of traditions and practices, herbal magick should not be seen as the stereotypical cackling woman stirring a big cast iron pot of green potion, but rather as the cultivation of deep reverence for the spirit and natural world, while forging a healing bond with the healing powers of plants.

As energy is neither created nor destroyed, it is in the science of its transference that helps to supply aid for physical affliction or simply incite healing. Clarity with sincerity is the energetic link between plant life and the intended outcome of said magick. Energy is the vital source that animates all existence in the practice of herbal magick. It flows through the universe binding the realms of spirit to living matter. In this context, energy is the medium for intention and the catalyst for spiritual transformation.

Corresponding with the physical, emotional, and spiritual properties of the human being are the unique fingerprints of the energetic signatures of plant life. This fundamental force shapes all creation, while energy follows the efforts of intention. Whatever energy is expelled into a ritual is directed by the pure will of the practitioner. It is the essence of magickal feats divinely wielded through high levels of consciousness. Practitioners attune themselves to the vibrational sensitivities of plants while manipulating energies to amplify their intentions. To cultivate awareness of the very subtle frequencies and currents of nature is the very thing that leads one to become a masterful herbalist.

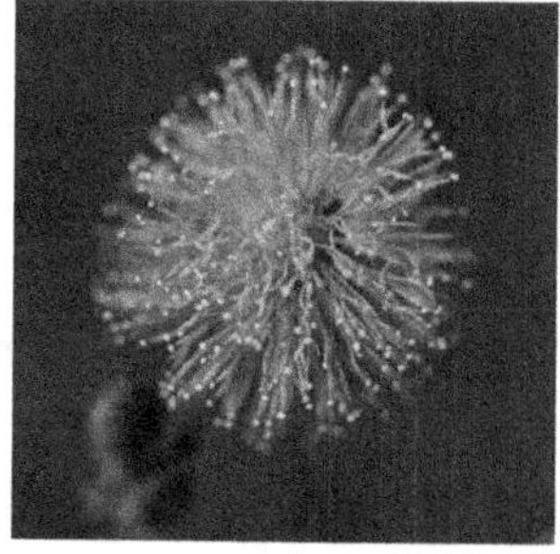

Conscious will nourish the mechanical balance of holistic healing through practice. The imbalances of the physical are the composition of what is perceived as sick. This perception is the basis of experimentation for practitioners. It has also propelled significant medical findings in practice. Ultimately this logic perpetuates an individualized impression of the magick of herbalism.

In the prisms of natural sciences, the gesture of intention is only forceful when the direction of energy is concise. Remember that even at rest we are constantly in motion at a cellular level. So what if we consider the same for the practice of herbal magick? It's safe to say that without the energy of intent in herbal medicine, remedies are made from a hope, a wish, and a prayer. Herbalism must generally be about relating plant vitality and its energy to the imbalances of the individual or ailment. Once in tune with the energies of the individual being serviced, master herbalists can then make relative constitutions with the vigor of the appropriate herbs or plants.

In the belief that harmony can be found in the healing combination of plants, practices are meant to enhance the vital life force. Intention to optimum vitality is to be met on both ends of the practice, in regard to herbalist and client. The magick remains in the manipulation of energies. Underlying the transformative rituals that promote healing, energy imitates the level of consciousness of the mind.

When the rhythm of nature communes with energies of intention, the song is of high healing frequency. A deep organic connection to the natural properties of plant life is seen as a spiritual connection to the universe. The strengthening of this connection is ongoing and requires mindful experimentation. The magick used by healing practitioners is in direct correlation to the energetic properties of the herbs or plants they experiment with. Some may describe this interaction as the natural phenomenon of the practice.

As botanists study to identify the function of flora and the variation of species, herbalists study to influence their properties holistically. In this case, they have dedicated themselves to bringing natural healing remedies to the African American community, which can be inclusive of spiritual guidance or holistic support. Plants with healing DNA attribute to the medicinal effects of herbal magick. Herbalism categorizes these attributes by elemental interactions, such as earth, fire, air, and water. Think of these elements as the shepherds of virtue in the openness of natural forces. As mint tea cools the fire within, sage embers burn a sense of calm into any space. Applied magick finds support in the energetic qualities of the elements.

Furthermore, a professed interconnected ardor for the wonder of plants is seen as a form of spiritual projection. It is supplemented by the divine secrets of the elements and consequently nurtured as a form of enlightenment. To say it is an extraordinary commitment to discovery is an understatement. The dedication necessary to understand the holistic value of plant properties must result in a rendering brilliance of interpreting the imbalances and impressions of the natural world. Grappling with the charms of flora imposes natural law upon the practitioner. A self-sovereignty that empowers the healer to encourage transformation with preventative holistic care.

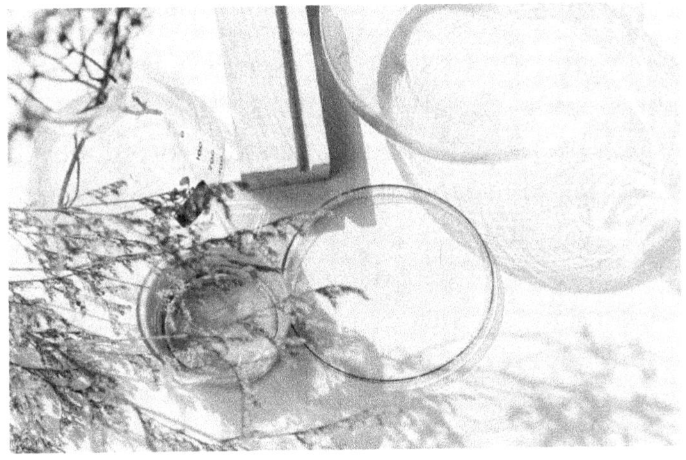

Plants are sometimes classified in accordance with astrological alignment, their correspondences, and magickal properties. Palo santo, formally known as cedarwood, is an earth element often used for spiritual protection and ritualistic prayer to open the space to receive messages from the ancestors. Adding heat to cedarwood ensures groundedness, a sense of stability, and calm. Take ginger and cinnamon as another example, both of the fire element and known to employ transformation and passion and assist in the rapid fire of synapses. By understanding their magickal properties relative to the forces of the universe, healers can create synergy with natural law, harnessing protection, love, and divination. Integrating correspondences amongst plants is seen as a harmonious act deepening one's connection to the magick.

As the essence of these practices lives within the energies of intention, the herbalist's relationship with plants must be profound. It must be an ever-written haiku of wonderment; a deep respect that honors the spirit of the plant and the privilege of its existence. This is an essential principle in practice as one learns how to transcend beauty into remedy. It's a bond of gracious humility and intelligence.

Natural law calls for practitioners or healers to encourage reciprocity and consciousness of the plant kingdom. Cultivating a relationship with the environment that reveals the ancient tools for optimum health requires respect. Translating to an ethical harvest of plants while engaging in sustainable practice is implored by genuine appreciation aside from acquired skill. From understanding the potency of the herb to the volatility of its effects when it is misrepresented in a remedy, a dedicated practitioner remains a lifelong student. Communing with flora confirms the energetic signature formed when appreciation is shown to the unique gifts of the Earth.

A sacred space for spiritual growth and evaluation finds itself adamantly within the sanctuary of African American herbalism. Wildcrafting a magikal garden of healing and supplemental herbs is an intimate act. From the fertilization of soil to the gentle upkeep of the blossom, flora must be cared for attentively. The natural world must have a balance of the elements to be fully activated in power. It is with this knowledge that practitioners engage in a personal trek of self-discovery. One that is resolute in natural law and motivated by the needs of others, cultivating purpose through discovery.

Many are misled by misinformation, mostly due to a lack of research or resources. However, holistic healing has proven to be much more than just an alternative to Western medicine. Natural healers must be connected to spirit and nature with a healthy understanding of natural properties. They must be attuned to energies with the wisdom to manipulate the elements to support the influence of plant varieties. A divine union of consciousness and creation nourishes the fundamental idea of healing in magickal herbalism.

Emphasis on the power of intention is meant to harness balance in ritual or ground the practitioner to purposeful services. Principles of African American herbalism remind us humans that gratitude is a must; that energy flows even from person to plant and this exchange is symbiotically influenced by one another. Directing this flow toward the desired relief of sickness, sadness, anxiety, or other imbalances is a lifetime of exploration. As the principles in Western medicine lean towards suppression rather than cure, herbal medicine is a soulful practice of the universal kind. The focus is balance for optimum health and higher consciousness. Herbal magick carves the path for high potential in the transformative light of any individual who partakes in its wisdom, whether master herbalist, basic practitioner, or client.

Magick in the context of herbalism is a combination of energetic forces. Intention, energy, and sensitivity to the natural law of flora are the principles of herbal magick. The subtle  energies of each little hair on the sage leaf or fiber from the cinnamon bark are interconnected and honored in the proverbial book of herbal magick.

Its velvety texture and silvery-green-hued stalk are distinctive of the physical properties of sage. Much like its role in the spiritual practice of magick. Often used as a tool for spiritual cleansing of negative energies, sage is revered for its purification properties. A conduit of a potent release of energy, every tiny little hair on the sage leaf is proof lends to the importance of a conscious interconnected will to practice knowledgeably.

Imperceptible to the naked eye or the less-than-open consciousness, these subtle energies are where magick is built. Summoned through the effort of connectivity, we must acknowledge that magick is a repository of wisdom and power. As we swim into the depths of ritual and explore the seas of action in practice, allow this read to serve a purpose in your own spiritual development. Let this newfound knowledge decalcify your pineal gland while facilitating substance in your experience, as it is very much a personal one. We'll take the next chapter to highlight sacred plants and some of their ancestral uses, inviting you to further explore the natural tools used in remedy and ritual. The planet kingdom has over 120,000 species of flora that survive in the vast web of existence. The masterful practitioner of this healing science must invoke detailed knowledge to explain herbal concoctions when sought after for their natural services. Their bond with plants must transcend the boundaries of mainstream knowledge and honor the eternal smile of plant life.

CHAPTER 3
SACRED PLANTS AND HOLISTIC USE

The Earth keeps a powerhouse arsenal of plants that can either be helpful or harmful to humans. They can be poisonous or simply aesthetically pleasing to any of the five senses. They can calm anxious thoughts while clearing the body of infection. Each plant has a unique biochemical makeup that possesses compounds that can be manipulated in a variety of ways. Contrary to popular assumption, herbs are not superfluous in their existence.

As history and lore shed light on how much plants were heavily relied upon in past generations, we must also bring awareness to the variety of ways the plant kingdom has served us well. That same strange plant that grew widely in your grandmother's garden as a kid still exists. However, the knowledge behind how that plant works is much more comprehensive today.

The treasures of vitamins, minerals, and life-sustaining nutrients are embedded in plant DNA. Ancestral wisdom teaches us that herbs have long been a central source of remedy generations before our existence. Herbal medicine was a cherished secret kept by the enslaved, the former enslaved, and those who were forced to live off the land in servitude. As a wisdom rooted in culture and circumstance, African American herbalism and magick keeps Mother Earth in high esteem. Botanicals are used in ointments, incense, tinctures, teas, salves, you name it. An extensive lore of nature is all a part of ancestral tradition.

From fertile land to the perfect position on the kitchen windowsill facing east of the beams of sunlight, plants absorb the qualities of their location of growth. Herbs pull nutriment from their surroundings to compose a wealth of virtuous beauty from root to stem, to stalk. Sacred plants provide protection, healing, and spiritual empowerment even before harvest. The stimulating elements of natural law emanate within each living plant.

As frequencies vibrate the highest from freshly pulled herbs, beauty meets a sense of well-being in the bush. Fields of oat straw, ginger root, and elderberries can be seen as an enchanted garden of fortifying herbs that prevent illness. Imagine a meadow of calendula, dandelion, and lavender leading to you the grassy knoll of longevity in natural charm. What better way for practitioners to honor the efforts of the souls that have passed? A diverse botanical landscape to call your own, without borders or enforced boundaries. The honor is in the freedoms of exploration, practice, and choice.

Being careful not to overlook their validity, this chapter will focus on the sacred plants that are lesser known today but just as powerful as they were when used in ancestral herbal magick. Natural healing cannot be bound by the insecurities of man or else it simply will not work. So, let's spend some time going over a few sacred plants, their medicinal power, spiritual properties, and some uncommon uses. We will also embrace the sustainable practices of how to grow them and ethically wildcraft in diverse landscapes. In the bloom of the maypop tree, you can find the most compelling beauty as a reason to fully engulf yourself in the beauty of this very unusual perennial.

Maypop

Scientifically known as *Passiflora incarnata*, the maypop, otherwise known as the passionflower, produces edible fruit and holds a long history in antebellum herbalism. This fruit should not be confused with the tropical passion fruit plant found in Brazil as you would find this perennial vine in the southeast part of the United States. *Passiflora* means passionflower and the word *incarnata* translates to "in the flesh". The Powhatan Native Americans called it "maracock". In some parts of South Florida, they are said to bloom in May, but the seeds do  not grow large enough for you to step on and "pop" them until around June or July, hence the name maypop.

Maypop is a wild fruit that can take form in partial shade with good lighting and evenly moist soil. It germinates first into a hollow green egg shape which then ripens to fill with jelly and seeds, turning yellow on the outside. Vines trail and grow long with three-lobed leaves appearing from each bud. Leaves do sometimes sprout five lobes. This deciduous plant is herbaceous and grows to be about 30 feet in length with long climbing tendrils that grow 8–12 feet in height. It produces extrafloral nectaries at the base of its leaves.

Becoming orange as it matures, late summer brings shrubs of fruit that have a thick, yet spongy outer rind When it ripens seeds become unattached from the flesh on the inside. Flowers are white to lavender colored and distinctive. Petals are crimped purple filaments that wave along in the rhythms of the wind. Harmoniously centered are the pistol as well as five stamina—yellow-toned with purplish speckling. This vine produces beaucoup fruit when well maintained.

Medicinal and Spiritual Properties

The magick in this plant goes far beyond its exotic beauty as it was commonly used in traditional daily practice during slavery. While acknowledged as a sedative and most effective for nervous conditions, this beautiful wildflower wears many medicinal hats in ancestral healing. Berries are dried and used to treat restlessness. The extract depresses motor nerves and causes an immense feeling of relaxation. Although it is not recommended for the expecting mother. Studies show that it can help improve cognitive concentration while simultaneously treating anxiety.

Ancestral lore speaks of the maypop as a source of nutrition, helping to heal physical ailments and bring a sense of spiritual balance. This sweet and tangy fruit was known to bring relief to stomach ailments, high blood pressure, and hormonal symptoms of menopausal women. When juiced it cradles vitamin A, potassium, fiber, magnesium, and vitamin C. Emma Dupree mentioned that she had the pleasure of picking the fruit to add to the pancakes she made for her mother in the mornings. As it is high in niacin, the leaves can also be enjoyed raw or cooked. Leaves are paired with the flower itself for cooking or making syrup.

Herbalists also use maypop to treat urinary tract infections. The stems and leaves cradle antispasmodic properties, relieving symptoms of asthma while also serving as a vasodilator, hypnotic, and diaphoretic. It treats infections with antimicrobial compounds and alleviates withdrawal from opiates as well as recedes dependence on benzodiazepines. Aside from treatment for physical sickness, its daily use comes with a vast sea of nutritional benefits.

It is said that the maypop opens up the individual to spirit and natural wonder by easing irritability. This plant is a known herbal conductor of spiritual energies. It helps the mind to attune to the higher universal frequencies and to sharpen spiritual connections. Psychic abilities can be found in the essence of its flower while the vines and roots create a gateway for one to find release of stagnant energies. Ancestral practitioners believed manipulating the passionflower gave off such an intensity of vital energy that karmic purpose seeps itself into the inner workings of your chakras.

Cultivation

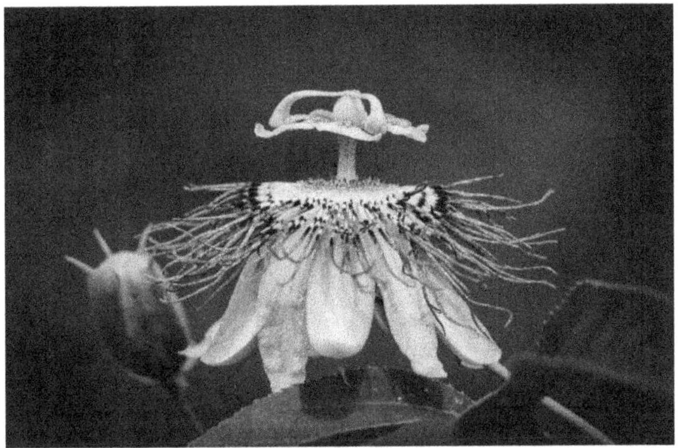

Maypop is an evergreen climber that has been seen growing along fenced rows, fields, open soils, or sandy tree-lined thickets where the soil is fertile and reliably moist. It has the ability to survive cold temperatures of 41 °F. This perennial thrives in full sun but will tolerate partial exposure. The best chance of its survival is to keep it sheltered from direct sunlight as to avoid scorching of the leaves.

Grown from a seed or root cuttings and relatively easy to cultivate. Root cuttings are said to promote faster, reliable growth in full sun. Cuttings take about 3 months to root and will do so aggressively. It will need to be pruned for optimum growth.

Seeds need to be presoaked in lukewarm water for 12 hours to be sown indoors in the late winter or early spring. Germination takes about 1–12 months, though one can expect flowering around June or July. The roots love mulch as it protects them from harsh temperatures, assists with water retention, and reduces weed competition.

The Ethical Harvest

There are a couple of obvious ways to harvest maypops. You can wait for them to drop to the ground or simply pluck the ripe ones from the vine. The color will reveal its ripeness, and slight pressure from the gentle press of your fingers will validate.

Harvest maypop in mid to late summer while it's in bloom. When gathering, only take the parts above ground that are the most mature. You must be careful to cut the vine at ground level so as to not disturb future growth from the roots. Once gathered, the plant is prepared by removing all foreign matter. Then the fruit is removed from the leaves to eat or smash. It is important to note that if fruit is left whole after harvesting it will mold and possibly ruin the rest of the harvest. The pulled leaves and flowers will crumble completely in about a week depending on drying conditions.

Mugwort

Ancestral healers hailed this plant as a magical herb and one of the most sacred in the practice of African American magick. Traditionally used for parasitic infection and a "tonic for the soul," its sweet, herbaceous essence is said to keep you aware of your spiritual direction. *Artemisia vulgaris* is a member of the daisy subfamily with whitish hairs and dark green leaves that are underlined with silvery plant veins. Naturalizing in North America, it remains a very accessible medicinal herb.

An ancient herb personifying warmth and strength, mugwort treats digestive disorders and respiratory issues and is used to encourage or maintain skin vitality. It also induces digestion and the absorption of nutrients while increasing appetite. As an antiseptic, mugwort was used to treat malaria and, when turned into a salve, is an effective antifungal or antibacterial treatment. It can be used as an insect repellent or the main ingredient in absinthe and brewed into beer.

One of its many pseudonyms, "the mother of herbs," substantiates its proven ability to regulate the female reproductive system as it stimulates the uterus. From alleviating cramps during menses, bloating, headache, diarrhea, and constipation to easing the pains of childbirth. This herb was certainly in the healing satchels of enslaved midwives. It remains in high regard amongst African American healers today, giving insight as to why some refer to it as "the old woman." Associated with feminine energies and ancestral wisdom, mugwort is said to bolster communications to the spirit world as lore tells it.

Mugwort is one of the most spiritually empowering plants to grace this earth.  Practitioners place bundles of this herb under their pillow for lucid dreaming or protection against bad entities that enter through dreams. It can be smoked, steeped in tea, or extracted for its essence. Note that mugwort contains a compound, called thujone, that causes psychoactive episodes of hallucinations and convulsions. However, it is generally safe in responsible doses and cross-culturally used in ritualistic practices.

Cultivation

Mugwort is a hardy perennial that grows in clumps and knows that once planted, it's there forever. It can be found anywhere: in parks, waste grounds, roadsides, streams, and even as shrubbery along riverbanks. This plant has the ability to thrive in a wide range of soil types, but holistically you want to nurture it in soil that has high alkalinity. Its flora has a preference for full sun but can survive in partial shade.

Blossoming without petals from a seed, it smells of minty sage with mild grassy notes. Stretching only 2–5 ft tall, this plant can grow aggressively in undisturbed areas. The weed of weeds, if you will. Seeds should be sown close to the surface of the soil in the early parts of spring. Flowering occurs around late summer while bloom is expected in late fall. As mugwort appreciates plenty of moisture, be careful to not overwater them. Too much water will cause root rot. Stems may begin to flop in high heat, though if well-established, is quite tolerant. If propagating, do so via basil cuttings when new growth starts to show.

The Ethical Harvest

Although mugwort is most commonly harvested in the fall, you can start picking leaves at soft growth in early spring. It all depends on how the practitioner depends on using the plant. Because of its wild growth, pruning is encouraged through the growing season and again during the coldest temperatures. In late summer the stem will thicken and can be hung to dry for use by the peaks of winter.

Sassafras

Native to the eastern parts of North America, sassafras grows quickly to be a medium-sized aromatic tree. Growing the largest in the Great Smoky Mountains, *sassafras albidum* reaches 3–10 ft in height and grows into a deciduous tree that loves open fields. All parts of this tree are aromatic with leaves 3 to 4 in. long. Dried leaves are commonly used in cooking, specifically in gumbo. It is then known as filé, a thickening agent for soups or gravy in Creole cooking. Teas are made from its leaves and used as a blood purifier. It is highly revered as a blood tonic and a trusted treatment for heart problems.

Ancestral use includes using oils from the

bark to make soups, root beer, and even chewing gum. The oil carries a pungency much like the smell of cinnamon. Ancestral wisdom suggests that it can be used to treat almost any ailment. Bark infusions were said to relieve joint pain from a long day of fieldwork as well as treat scarlet fever, smallpox, and measles. Its roots were made into cough medicine, mouthwash, and a gargle for colds. Another essential in the midwife satchel was sassafras root, used to treat a mother's fever post-childbirth. Healers would prepare this root into a poultice to be applied to a sprained ankle, bee stings, an open wound, and minor abrasions.

A spring tonic or blend made from its bark is said to be fantastic for bladder pain or gallbladder stones. Steeped bark was used to treat syphilis. Its sacred wood is still used in construction and furniture, making it a charmingly flexible resource for a holistic lifestyle. Powerful and a sight to behold during the turning of leaves for fall, some traditions spoke of its spiritual properties of bringing wealth and good luck to your life. With a broad spectrum of healing powers, it is used for shamanic protection or spiritual safety as if its physical qualities manifest into a spiritual purpose for the practitioner. Brewing the bark was also known to remove curses or the effects of dark spirits.

Cultivation

This tree is what they call dioecious—its male and female parts are on separate trees. The optimum pH of the soil is 6.0 to 7.0, but it can thrive even in poor soil. Through cloning of its lateral root system, the mother tree sends rootlets to the ground to feed as a new tree. Loving the full sun, it does not do well in dark forest spaces but will take partial exposure. They can adapt to sandy soil, though like any other plant, it grows best in the most fertile of dirt.

Seeds are produced about every other year once the tree has matured to 10 years. It should only be gathered once the fruit turns the color of dark blue. To plant, one must chill seeds at 41 °F for 120 days before allowing them to germinate underground. Sow seeds in moist, loamy soil in late fall with a protective leaf cover. Expect prolific sprouting with lateral growth and dense thickets. Note that these beauties do not transplant well if purchased as a youthful plant. Prunings are best during the winter months to remove dead wood, much like how one would exfoliate the skin for a vibrant glow.

The Ethical Harvest

Harvesting fallen roots is less of a disturbance to the larger part of the tree. This can be done easily between a seedling tree and the mother tree. As the inner bark is the most medicinal, it is wise to look for larger roots. Be sure to peel and remove the bark to fully capture the dynamic of its essence.

Coneflower

Otherwise known as Sampson root, the enslaved African American people learned of the glory of this plant from the indigenous healers of North America. It is said that the Choctaw and Delaware-Oklahoma tribes taught of echinacea's use as a stimulant of the immune system. Coneflower is a plant that can be used for teas and poultices, even when dormant during the coldest temperatures of the winter season.

This delightful wildflower, *E. purpurea,* is native to North America and is a part of the daisy family. The purple coneflower is the most common and accessible. Growing to the measurements of about 2 to 4 inches in diameter,  it is a sight during midsummer bloom when the disk of purple flowers gathers around a mounded, brown-centered cone. The leaves of this hard perennial are dark green. They grow closest to the ground at about 4 to 8 inches and stems sprout prickly. A meadow of these lovely coneflowers is said to be awe-inspiring upon sight.

Traditionally this plant was used to treat gastrointestinal issues, burns, toothaches, and fevers. Teas were made from the roots and purple flowers to relieve menstrual cramps and spasmodic complaints. Tradition finds an abundance of power in the root of this plant. Its nickname, Sampson root, is derived from its thick black roots, pungent taste, and powerful efficacy. This specific variety of echinacea, *e. purpurea*, has the least recorded findings out of the species. Research also suggests that it was only used to treat a minimal amount of conditions. The spirit and healing efficacy of this plant are no less valid because of the lack of scientific recording. It was also used in the treatment of syphilis and rattlesnake bites and is a prime ingredient in snake oil. Ancestors would take the plant pulp, crush it in between stones, and use the poultice to heal wounds.

Cultivation

Coneflowers are tolerant of drought. They require well-drained soil and prefer the warmth of full sun. Seeds should be planted 12 to 15 inches under the soil. They grow best when soul coverage is mixed with a thin layer of compost or manure. Germination takes place within 8 to 10 weeks if grown indoors. When plants are seed-sown outdoors, full bloom could take up to three years. Water from the soil level only so as to not cause fungal disease to the leaves. If soldier beetles appear on the plant in August, they should not be disturbed as they pollinate plants.

The Ethical Harvest

A pair of sharp sheers should be used to snip flowers when petals begin to expand. Harvesting can commence following the second year of growth. Roots are excavated with a garden fork or large shovel.

Goldenseal

Distinctively graceful by the sight of its thick, yellow-knotted rootstock, goldenseal's dry root is commonly paired with echinacea to prevent colds. It is one of the most popular herbal remedies throughout the history of African American herbalism. Extracts help to treat hay fever, sore gums, and digestive issues. *Hydrastis canadensis* is also used in many over-the-counter treatments such as laxatives, allergy relief pills, and eyewash formulations. This plant is rich in alkaloid compounds and was traditionally used for its antibacterial and inflammatory properties. For modern-day use, goldenseal is recommended by herbalists to help your body detox from toxins and harmful substances, helping you to eliminate said toxins through urine or sweat.

Cultivation

Ordinarily found growing on forested slopes in open woodlands, or along stream banks, goldenseal is at high risk of extinction. Densely clustered patches grow along the eastern half of North America, from Southern Ontario to Northern Georgia. It is slow-growing as an herbaceous perennial. Plants remain in the seedling stage for 1–2 years and then enter a juvenile stage of development. This phase could last up to two years before observing plant maturity. Finally, plants start to reproduce after 4–6 years of growth. It will sprout a fork stem with two leaves and 5–7 lobes. The smallest leaf will bear a little white flower, unfurling in April. Capable of self-fertilization, the fruit ripens mid- to late- July. Roots become fibrous and swell to birth a new plant.

Goldenseal grows best in well-aerated loamy soil with good water drainage. Its aggressive soil disturbance is usually harmful to neighboring plants, though ironically able to reduce disease in a mixed plant bed. Other species that grow best adjacent to it include red oak, slippery elm, and mayapple.

Outdoor sown seeds need to be naturally exposed to warmer temperatures in the late summer for a happy invasive germination the following spring. Goldenseal could also be propagated using portions of the fibrous root. Typically sown in a nursery bed, in-wood cultivated plants and their seedlings should be permanently transplanted after about two years of growth. Regardless of the approach, furrows should be dug about 2 inches deep to allow roots to spread laterally.

The Ethical Harvest

Goldenseal should be harvested in late fall as its leaves begin to fade. This also increases the medicinal properties of the roots. Roots should be washed thoroughly before use. It may help to soak them in a bowl of cool water to loosen up any hard debris. Contact with water should be brief to avoid the loss of any alkaloids. Refrain from having the water turn yellow to avoid this.

Horehound

Written records of slaves mention horehound as a bittersweet tea, candy, and cough syrup that alleviated sore throat. Paired with narrowleaf plantain, Marrubium vulgare was employed in Doctor Caesar's antidote for snake poison. It was also included in the treatments of earaches, infections, rashes, and cirrhosis of the liver. Modern-day herbalists still use it in cough drops and as an ingredient in the relief of bronchitis, hypertension, and diabetes. Leaves can also make insecticide when mixed with milk.

Naturalized in North and South America in the 19th century, the roots and leaves have been used in cough medicines since ancient Egyptian times. It is commonly known as white horehound and is a part of the mint family. Its leaves are oval with a grayish-green stem and jagged edges below the flower whorl. Puckered at about 1.5 inches long with white wooly hairs and wrinkled tops., the stems grow to be about 3 feet tall, woolly, and four-sided. Flowers are tiny and tubular at about 1/4 inch long where the leaf meets the stem.

Cultivation

Horehound is a highly fragrant herb that makes a bitter, yet pleasant-tasting healing juice. This perennial blossoms a white flower in midsummer. It forms a dense root system with large monocultures that are difficult to eradicate, creeping upright like a shrub with a pungent aromatic odor. Each flower produces one seed with four dark brown nutlets and fibrous, branched roots. It grows in disturbed places at 2,000 to 8,000 feet of elevation. It can be seen alongside roads, in deserts, mountains, upland, and riparian.

Due to the fact that it spreads over large areas, plant diversity will be reduced. Horehound should be planted in well-drained soil in early spring as a seedling or transplanted into the soil from a houseplant. Seeds should be sown about 1/4 deep into the Earth and 10 inches apart from each other. Seeds will be slow to germinate and need consistent moisture.

The Ethical Harvest

Mature plants should be dug out by the roots.

A Power That Spans Generations

These plants are a powerful few that sustained life during brutal circumstances. They continue to hold sacred space in the practices of African American herbalism and magick. The space they occupy is quite special and significant in past lives. Spiritual healers today look to these herbs in reverence of ancestral wisdom and what is 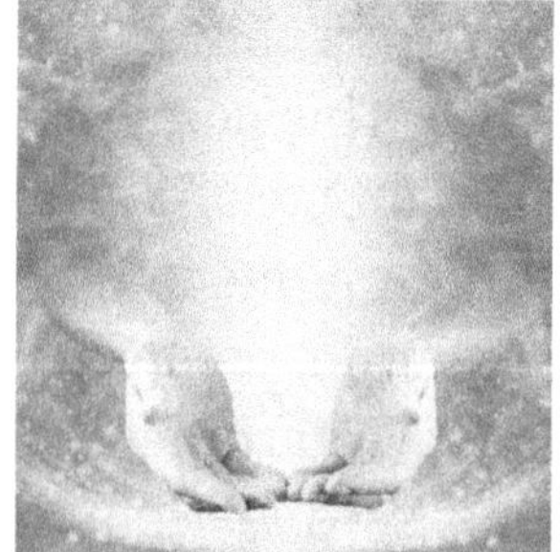 considered magickal healing. From mugwort's ability to induce a trance to using the pith of a sassafras plant to dress a burn, combined with the elements each plant transcends physical treatment, each giving way to spiritually shape the healer into embracing the deepest connection of plants to medicine.

CHAPTER 4
THE ART OF ANCESTRAL COMMUNICATION AND DIVINATION

What is ancestral communication and divination?

We must first understand the terms relative to the African American diaspora. Ancestral refers to the lineal or inherited wisdom of those who lived before us. In this case, we refer to the offspring of a people who were stolen from their homeland of Africa and forced to migrate to a foreign place and give free labor. Transatlantic journeys were a stamp in time when ancient African traditions met the imposition of traditional practices of the Western world. In African tradition, belief is in the ubiquitous spirit of the ancestors and the omnipresence of The Creator. As it was forbidden to partake in practices of their homeland in the New World, the life of a slave was dangerously interwoven with spirituality and the ancestors revered amongst spirit. These people were the first set of African Americans: a set of people now generalizing all people of color, no matter their ethnic origin, who live in North America.

An ancestor is typically one's direct relative of the past, though in this chapter we will continue to generalize the reference for the sake of exploring unexamined views and disrupting historic presumptions. Relatively, we shall define divination as using one's intuition to attune to any occurrence, then using nature or natural forces and the elements to influence said circumstance. This type of passed-down knowledge translates to the holistic gifts and behaviors of most spiritual healers. Culturally it would be most apropos to seek the guidance of ancestors or a masterfully spiritually inclined being, as it was believed that illnesses could be of the natural or supernatural variety.

Ancestral communication is the art of keeping in touch with the forerunners of your existence. Abetting the struggle and breathing life into the legacy of lost homes is an act that truly honors the lives and experiences of past generations. It is a divine right and, as a healing practitioner, one serves as a medium between celestial energies, plant life, and the sick.

Maintaining a strong connection to the spiritual world serves as a means to gaining insight, occupying a sacred space for healers. There are tools and techniques that amplify the energy exchange in this sacred space. This exchange is fuel for ancestral communication.

Divination is used in respect to those who have studied energy to master the use of divine connection between the healer and the elements. It's a consultive institution with individualized extremes. Fundamental belief is in the bountiful abilities of nature and the channeling of powerful energies for manipulation into discipline or ritual. Britannica describes divination as a tradition for a body of organized specialists (Britannica, 2024). Though it is a fact that any common individual can host an incomparable rolodex of divinatory specialties as a diviner, the concept has historically been misconstrued with arbitrary association with witchcraft, the dark occult, or sorcery.

Ancestral communication and divination bridge the gap between the physical and spiritual realms. Insight into the interconnectedness of the metaphysical is revealed exclusively through personal experience and spiritual enlightenment.

Spirituality is a discipline that cannot be taught but can be heightened by conscious guidance and coveted clarity.

Because divination takes the form of the device used to bring forth its effects, it may employ inexplicable phenomena. Diviners implore refined skill when harnessing this combination of intuitive and interpretative practices. Rooted in ancient traditions, African American divination encompasses a wide range of tools. Practice ranges from the casting of bones, leaves, 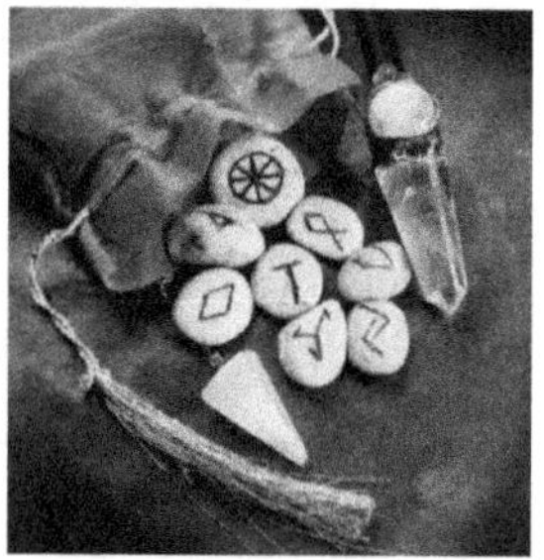 or stones, to the use of herbs collectively with universal forces and the five elements. Let's further explore the tools, methods, and spiritual significance of ritualistic practice.

Important Spiritual Significance

Ancestors would sometimes use stones and bones to diagnose and prescribe treatment for various psychological, psychiatric, and spiritual conditions. Reduced to primitive superstition, it is important to remember that these traditions and remedies were remnants of ancient African practices. Keep in mind that those forced to migrate to North America had to adapt to the natural environment. However life-threatening, the belief in the outcome of these practices is the very thing that healers reflect upon in homage to their ancestors. Just having the freedom to reflect in gratitude is a form of communication within itself. It celebrates the ancestor's belief that communication with spirit is a birthright. One of the ways practitioners celebrate such is by spiritual healing or treating illnesses of the living.

Traditional Methods Explained

Discovering hidden knowledge within the practice of spiritual healing is the essence of the divine. It straddles the line of artistic expression and assembles quality results when execution is of the highest integrity. Quality often depends on the type of limitations imposed (if any) and the types of instruments designed for divinatory quests. Spiritual instruments are of common variety in many ancient belief systems, especially throughout Africa, and are valuable in practice.

No matter the type of tool or spiritual law behind its nature, the basic principles for any divination device are the same. One must choose a set of symbolic objects that have deeper meaning than what's in plain sight. Often indicative of efficacy in long traditions, these objects are placed in patterns of symbolism amongst or between symbolic objects that personify connection to energies. The object is meant to help the diviner discover meaning or interpret the relationship of energies between the items of significance, regarding circumstance and the intention of assembly.

Traditional spiritual healers find that they have a special calling that leads them to guide or heal others through divination work. This suggests that divination is a system of beliefs grounded in intention or magick that is unpredictable. It alludes that all that we need for survival as humans can be found within the complements of Earth. Opportunity for healing presents itself as a constant in nature., aiding us in managing the relationship between the human mind, body, and spirit. It helps us to navigate the complexities of the spirit world, the laws of nature, and astute consciousness.

There isn't such a thing as a user's manual for interpreting bones, casting stones, or any other divine practice, but for the sake of debunking myths and clarifying misinterpretations, we will explore a few of these methods used to consult with the ancestors more in depth.

Throwing Bones

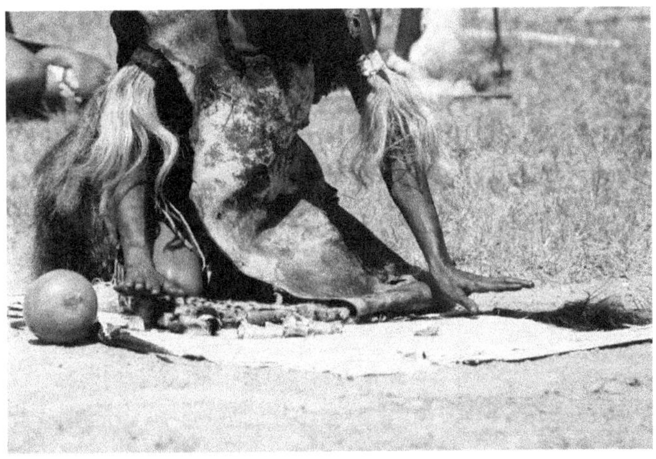

One of the oldest divine methods dates back to ancient times. It was one of the many skills of traditional healers in southern parts of Africa, used in the Xhosa, Swazi, Ndebele, and Zulu tribes. Consulting the ancestors with the vertebrae of animals is otherwise known as osteomancy in modern day. More than just bones can be tossed in the mix for a reading or interpretation of patterns: Relative to any object that the diviner appoints special meaning, animal bone, shells, or seashells are cast and thrown piece by piece in a collection on a hard surface. The hard surface is blessed and dressed in circular or casting cloth. Often times the casting cloth is inscribed or inked with symbols and virtuous prompts, serving as a spiritual compass of sorts. Herbalists may even draw a simple circle in the loose ground with a stick as opposed to cloth. Burning mugwort, sage, and other intention-setting botanicals sets the tone and clears the chosen space for channeling energies to communicate with the ancestors. Anointing a candle with plant essence, lighting it, and placing it aside a glass of water next to your throwing surface will facilitate openness to receive messages from the spirit.

Household items, trinkets, charms, pendants, and the like can be used to substitute the bones as devices. This will only work if you are resolute in the meaning of the items. The people of the Caribbean and Brazil still practice using cowrie shells and 16 palm nuts. Ancestral wisdom teaches that everything has spirit.

The items should hold significance to you, to the circumstance, and to the intention, giving meaning to its less-than-random inclusion into the divination work. Meditating on the significance of the chosen items and the question you seek to be answered before initiating a reading is all a part of tradition. Meditation often included dance and song in ancestral times. Calling upon the ancestors should be loud and clear for divine insight.

Depending on where the item lands, or

rather its placement in the casting, will determine how to read and decipher the patterns—messages within the unseen ripples of space to be received. Interpretation is derived from where the items touch to the distance of placement from one object to another. There are no rules to what the diviner can use in place of bones and no step-by-step list for interpretation. This is the magick of it all: intuition. Spirit is an individual encounter or experience as is one's set of tools for divination. Said to go way beyond telling the fortunes of the future, the casting of bones is an excellent way to harness psychic power for illuminating your way to clarity. Overthinking this method will cloud reflection and observation of readings.

Stone Casting

Similar to casting bones, throwing small stones, crystals, or even pebbles can be used as conduits of divine guidance. Practitioners assign associated meanings to the stones according to their size, color, shape, texture, and elemental significance. Healers draw upon the elemental energies and inherent frequencies of the chosen stone. In some instances, the client and practitioner both cast stones one at a time. The healer will determine the metaphorical interpretation of the cast to best assist the client in their circumstance or ailment. A series of throws will tell the diviner what the ancestors require to help find resolve and what tools are necessary to support prognosis.

Crystals possess vibrational qualities that use energetic properties to influence divine insight. Common stones like quartz, selenite, amethyst, and jade are all quite accessible today. However, we  must consider the moment in time when mere field stones, blessed and referenced as rune stones in divination, were all that was available for certain indigenous groups. However, variations of this method are plentiful and quite personal of a choice.

Guidance from spirit in tradition is the idea that the human is a microcosm of opportunity. Throwing stones and reading the fallen arrangement is just as powerful as if one used bone, trinkets, or otherwise. A wide range of issues, from matters of the heart to the cause of blockage in spiritual harmony, can be dealt with through consultation with the spirit. Interpretations of the signs depend on cultural experiences, oral traditions, and depths of ancestral knowledge.

Herbal Divination

Involving the use of herbs exclusively is inclusive of healing botanicals of all kinds. Plants give us clear access to the guidance of the spiritual realm. Healers could have the gift of reading tea leaves or gaining intuitive insight by connecting the herb to the intention and using the elements to influence the outcome. Various herbs, dried leaves, roots, flowers, incense, infusions, or essential oils can be used as energetic carriers of divine purpose. Attuning to their attributes and corresponding properties allows for messages from the spirit to translate into practice. As Emma Dupree describes it, an acclimation of this kind is celestial and second nature to true healers. Herbal properties can enhance receptivity to messages from the great divine.

A vital role in African American herbalism, the connection to flora is an intensity that can't be learned, though it can be heightened through intuition and experience. Herbs serve as spiritual offerings, incense, and ritual-enhancing tools. Sage, rosemary, mugwort, lavender, and High St. John are just a few of the common ritualistic herbs relied upon for ancestral communication. Invoking presence through smoke and smudging facilitates awareness in a higher consciousness of psychic ability, attuning the practitioner to the energies of the natural world and taking honest advantage of the spirit.

Trance Dancing

Trance dancers are said to be chosen by spirit or ancestral deity during prayer or meditation. After being chosen, individuals dance in a hypnosis-like state. Almost functioning as an oracle, they can sift out problems of those in need and provide viable solutions for consideration. Not to be mistaken for the powers of sorcery, trance dancers seem to reach a state of enlightenment that allows the unseen to be seen and the silence to be heard. Conferring with the depths of the unknown is a distinction in simplified acts such as dance. The original association is with the Yoruba people of Nigeria, though corroboration of this practice parallels the cultures of the native inhabitants of the West Indies and North America.

Partaking in this particular modality is an expressive form of ancestral communication. Belief is in the rhythmic movement posing as the instrumental gateway to the conveyance of spiritual energies. This is a communal ritualistic institution of drumming and dance. Sound paired with rhythm are the essential components, or tools for the sake of the lesson, that mollify the effects of the mind into a trance state. The energy achieved through trance is channeled through an expressive flow of motion of the physical body. Traditionally drums beating at about 220 beats per minute are consecrated according to belief systems. Once engulfed in spiritual energies, the dancer emulates the characteristic of the dominant visiting spirit through a manifestation of movement or an unidentifiable tongue.

Some traditional practice summons the participation of the congregation. Gathered in concentric circles, they also dance to strengthen the energetic focal point. The tranced dancer is the focal point for distributing intention and once signs of spirit appear, the fellow communicants wait for the message to also reveal itself. Guidance is likely to come in the fashion of personal advice, warning for the population, reprimand, or guidance for the masterful. It is said that once the spirit leaves the conscious space, the tranced dancer does not remember the occurrence.

Ethical Responsibility

In practicing divination and ancestral communications, diviners must understand the importance of principle with respect to the tradition of ancient wisdoms. Reverence and integrity come hand in hand when attempting these methods. It is essential to approach divination as a sacred practice to bolster connection to the great divine by communicating with the spirit. Ancestors are relatives beyond bloodlines. Communicating with them helps one to stay connected to the Creator. It is believed the ancestors are message conveyors to the Great Divine with exclusivity.

Rituals executed with humility and sincerity acknowledge spirit with gratitude. Practitioners, diviners, or spiritual healers must embark on this journey to discovery with an open heart and an open mind. Exercise caution when attempting to manipulate energies to ensure intentions are pure and in alignment with laws of nature.

In the art of divination and ancestral communications, we honor this birthright with great aesthetic power. This power is animated through an instrument tapped with the potency of intention. All divination systems behold commonalities where understanding the terms of the present circumstance and questioning matters of the immediate future leads to resolution or healing epiphanies. This is, with the exception of one, discovering how long or prosperous life will be. Some new practitioners find it easier to understand relics through religion as religion is a source of comfort for the masses to share in belief systems. One should consider that all spiritual ideology involves stimulated perception and enlivening the senses. Diviners, spiritual healers, and herbalists carry forward the legacy of African American divination by embracing the wisdom and messages from ancestral communication, as well as enriching lives through servicing the community.

CHAPTER 5

IN THE SPIRIT OF COMMUNITY AND HEALING

Community plays a huge role in the human experience by shaping our existence and fostering relationships, all the while providing a feeling of support and belonging to a greater purpose. African American herbalism and magick cradle community with tools of natural law, healing, resilience, and collective transformation made available through ancestral guidance of spiritual discovery. Community in this sense is like sacred thread binding people together in a tapestry of shared purpose, facilitating healing and fostering resilience in the face of collective trauma or adversity.

To conceptualize African American Herbalism and Magick is to explore a level of consciousness that creates space for empathy and spiritual growth in discovering the unknown. It is understanding that the strength of a people dwells in the spirit of its community and that spirituality and relationships are of influential assistance in healing from traumatic events, whether it is healing oneself or being sought after to provide as a service to the people. African American tradition almost always finds prophetic resources in the social support of community, much like the land provides the actualization of healing energies through plant life.

The Role of Community in Healing

African American history starts with the traditions of ancient tribal people who were taken to foreign lands against their will. Taken to places where profit trumped ethics and humanity. With their families dismantled and lives sold to other human beings, it was the love of strangers sharing in dismal circumstances that helped to mitigate the demands of servitude.

Surrendering to the power of community is embracing a sense of consistency in the wealth of relationships. Often times in the African American community, these relationships are bound by the complex manifestation of ancestral dislocation. A connection that solidifies a deep acceptance of existence and hope for a harmonious future. To examine the unjust experiences of elders and to eat from the ancestral fruits of wisdom is acknowledgment that deep-rooted inequities can somehow create sovereignty amongst the marginalized. Situated between liberation and communal support, spiritual frameworks are nourished with camaraderie. In crucial times of hardship and adversity, community is a lifeline of empathetic solidarity that amplifies in the encounter of illness or challenges.

Communal Healing Through Herbalism

Deeply rooted in the wisdom of nature, herbalism is an unequivocal pathway to community healing. Giving a potent avenue of resilience in the belief that the natural will provide in abundance, herbalism has long been esteemed in communal practice. Traditions of plant-based medicine are passed down through generations as opposed to being recorded fluently in the medical journals of the modern Western world. In a time of crisis, herbalism serves the community in resilience, feeding all a sense of empowerment Expanding the concept of medicine beyond Western practices by incorporating indigenous flora is anchored by solidarity.

Leveraging the social inclination of healing through herbalism is in consideration of the importance of relationships, the most prominent one being the relationship between informal botany and spiritual disciplines that culturally encapsulates the power of community. The masterful African American herbalist is recognized by the community as a reliable healer to the masses with prevailing knowledge of spiritual propensity. Their affinity to the natural cultivates immense value to a people who have been stripped of origin.

Empress Karen M. Rose embraces the depths of communal herbalism with her Sacred Vibes Apothecary, which offers mentorship programs and apprenticeships. For the sake of helping others in their discovery of physical and spiritual identity, she has designed communal programs weaving ancestral knowledge with personal experiences, creating a sacred physical and emotional space for individuals to find their best selves amidst struggle or ailment. Rose has dedicated her life to advocating for spiritual traditions within the Afro-Caribbean and African American communities. Masterful in her craft, she offers guidance for those on a path of higher consciousness through the simplistic, yet divine use of herbs by encouraging clients to nourish mind, body, and soul.

Emma Dupree used the roots, leaves, fruits,

and flowers of her own herbal garden to sustain longevity in her personal life while caring for the sick in her neighborhood and family. She spoke of its abundance and how others would come and forage for fresh mint, maypop fruits, and sage. Modern community gardens, typically found in the inner cities, can be just as accessible and are affordable alternatives to traditional healthcare services. As the saying goes, it is better to prevent than to cure. These gardens are metaphorically rooted in a community taking control of their health by using holistic principles and cultural competency as convoy healing. By providing herbal consultations, spiritual wellness workshops, and herbal remedies to present-day practitioners, the grassroots initiatives of ancestors flourish. Addressing health disparities with cultural relevance empowers individuals to take part in collective dynamism.

Magick and Collective Transformation

As a catalyst for collective transformation and healing, magick harnesses the unseen forces of the universe through herbalism. The art is in employing the energies of spirit and the natural to work together to create change. This is a powerful tool for the community to render unwavering resilience and strength. When hardship presents itself as debilitating, magick has a way of shining an effervescent light of hope for those who seek wisdom for self-discovery in this realm, finding protection in this discovery as well as spiritual growth to permeate through the gritty life experiences of the collective.

Communal rituals and traditional ceremonies activate the powers of intention, which is an energy exchange that symbolizes how unity and sense of purpose can manifest a shift in mindset. Collective healing is not only a chance for personal transformation but also a golden opportunity for remembrance: remembering how colonial imposition forced the disconnect of ancient practices and induced the feeling of lost identity across generations; reflecting on cultural evolution and the untold stories of plant-based healers who integrated magick into their work; and reaffirming indigenous ways of belonging and the sacrament of healing forged with intention.

Congregating in a communal sacred space for spiritual observance to establish focal points of healing provides sanctuary for magickal connection and reverence collectively. Communal gatherings provide a nurturing space of peace that holsters ascension of vibrational intensities. Whether nestled in the heart of nature or carefully crafted within the gems of urban landscapes, community gatherings serve as a portal to the spirit of African American magick by offering a tangible representation of magick within the community while inviting practitioners to commune in sacred solidarity. Within these hallowed grounds, the veil between the physical and spiritual realms grows thin. It is a place where all who enter find guidance, solace, and inspiration in connectivity. Through solitary reflection, rituals, or ceremonies, practitioners honor the inherent sanctity of these spaces. Tapping into ancestral wisdom uses boundless collective energies that imbue the universe, and even the soul. By embracing the sanctity of these sacred spaces, the human will explore a higher level of consciousness and find forgiveness for the transgressions of others, or forgiveness of self. They will embark upon a journey of renewal and connection, transcending the limitations of ancestors.

With the goal of spiritual ascension, these types of practices usually call for a purified altar of sorts. As mentioned before, there are no rules to your pathway to spiritual balance. However, let's not forget that every culture has its traditions and ways of practice. In this regard, there is much misunderstanding and many misconceptions as to the use of altars as spiritual devices. Their spiritual significance is either oversimplified or misattributed. Contrary to the belief of the status quo, altars have an origin of serving as sacred spaces for ritual, prayer, and meditation in the African American magick culture. They are unique representations of the highest vibration and carry the intentions of the mind, body, and soul. Ancestral practices teach that when dressing the altar, the objects are considered sacred. Objects are prepared by being washed in purified water mixed with a few drops of essential oil and a bit of sea salt. Traditional practice calls for a white cloth to dry the objects. This could be because the color white is a prism for all colors, so it can logically be referenced in the same manner for the way it transcribes the energies or intentions of practitioners. Aside from burning, sipping, or wearing flower essence, a ritual of cleansing the sacred space with a cinnamon broom helps to set the tone for spiritual awareness.

Here is a list of sacred items traditionally used to adorn the altar and their typical purpose:

Tablecloth or Linen

- In modern-day adornment, it is common for practitioners to use traditional African prints, styles, and patterns for altar linen. But like any other magickal device, the focal point is on intention, not design. Other examples could be cloth representative of color chakras or, in some practices, colors are indicative of the type of guidance one seeks from spirit.

- Ancestral tradition calls for the table to be covered with a white, clean cloth that symbolizes purity. The air smells of frankincense and myrrh while call-and-response hand clapping catches the vibrations of the drum.

Baptism Bowl or Glass

- This device is filled with water and placed on the altar. Not only is it said to help absorb negative energy, it is a conduit for communication with the spirit world.

- Practice is to pour out the water after the completion of each ceremony. Community elders or spiritual leaders replenish the bowl before the commencement of the next session of divine work.

Pictures

- Pictures are typically of individuals who are of inspiration. In some cases, pictures of deities or figures of cultural divinity will be placed in frames made of natural material, usually made of wood, glass, or stone.

Plant Life

- Fresh-cut flowers establish energies of gratitude for the natural and interconnectedness with the vibrations of the living earth.
- An aloe plant or eucalyptus bundle are great examples of sacred plants to place upon the altar for the spirit of collective healing. Fresh sunflowers offer the energy of renewal and new beginnings. It could be a sacred addition to any altar.

Candles

- Tradition honors the fire element with the lighting of candles.
- Ancestral wisdom teaches that the color of the candle should correlate with the frequency of the energy one is trying to transmit.

Stones or Crystal

- Sacred altar stones or crystals harness the energies of minerals to further support healing intention while influencing the mindset.
- Belief is in the ability to alter the vibration of molecules of the body to match the reason for which they are being used, ultimately enhancing the body's healing process.
- They cultivate mindful meditation and work to align the chakras in preparation for spiritual advancement.

Food, Spices, and Fresh Fruit

- Sacred food is placed on the altar as offering to The Creator and the ancestors.
- Offerings should be high quality and fresh; they can consist of grains, fruit, or spices.
- Food is traditionally presented in a wooden or clay bowl, plate, or tray.

Libations

- Libations are placed on the altar as an offering to those who have passed on. Its primary significance is the act of pouring.
- They are commonly poured into a jug or shallow container of wine, milk, honey, rum, or bourbon.
- Sometimes libations are dispensed into the mouths of the commune and expelled over the altar, or simply poured from a vessel to sacred ground. This is a practice that continues to transcend time and cultures.

Other Sacred Symbols

- In modern-day practices, symbolic relics such as the ankh and the medicine wheel can be found centered amongst other sacred objects.
- As there are no rules, symbols can come in the form of beads, paintings, figurines, and drawings.
- Ancient practice likely used handmade items, jewelry, and even bird feathers that represent mind, body, and spirit.

Many in the modern world deem this magick as dark with the intention to bring harm to others or to conjure evil entities. However, it's quite the contrary: African American lore emphasizes how the community is energized by ritualistic gatherings where magick positively transforms the being while also giving individual perspective and fostering resilience to circumstance.

Cultivating Resilience and Belonging

A fundamental element of community is the reaffirming sense of belonging. Cherished especially in the worst of times, it provides a safe place for healing and discovery. Facing collective trauma and generational silence of heritage is an experience that is only truly  understood through personal experience. A conflicting feeling of comfort is found by socializing with others who can share in the discomfort of adversity. By coming together, the healing potential can be exponential. Action can be inspired from interaction and the impression that support is always accessible. Understanding is always available and all degrees of human existence can be palpable.

By coming together in shared intention, members of the community draw upon their birthright of the freedom to believe: to believe that there is truth in the lies of darkness. To believe that there is remedy to sickness and a place to find peace within despair. Drawing upon the counsel of the ancestors is a spiritual remedy for the weary. In this sense, the powers of the natural world navigate life's challenges and bid hope of a more just future for the community. Practices of African American magick and herbalism have a way of building common ground for the community to come together to process generational grief and share ancestral lore or tools that transcribe healing energies.

To illustrate the profound impact of herbalism and magick today in community, we must consider a people grappling with the systematic effects of oppression. Spiritual healers are left with a centuries-old responsibility of practicing herbal medicine to address illness, soothe emotional distress, and promote overall well-being.

The ebb and flow of existence can be relentless and unforgiving. If it were not for ancestral wisdom and resilience within the strength of community, the perils of African American history would perish in misconceptions and time. Herbalism and magick are tools of might that lend a hand in reclaiming agency over health and heritage, forging deeper connections with the natural world and individuals.

As we navigate the deep waters of the pernicious tendencies of humans, we draw inspiration from ancestral wisdom and the healing traditions of generations past to stay rooted in the procurement of harmony within the self. Community binds individuals together in shared purpose connection, and support. Empowering members of the community to heal, grow, and thrive together embodies the absolute resilience of the human spirit.

CHAPTER 6
TRADITIONAL HERBAL REMEDIES

The art of crafting tea, tinctures, salves, and tonics has long been venerated as remedies tailored to diverse health and spiritual needs. Traditions use the abundant bounty of the natural world which has given the herbalists of the African American diaspora a vast array of formulations and techniques to address common ailments, promote holistic living, and support spiritual inclination.

Much of modern medicine is but a chemical substitute for plant extracts. Countless pharmaceutical drugs are derived from the powerful compounds of nature. The ability to survive and heal using what is available at hand is all in the beauty of traditional herbal practices. While modern medicine has undoubtedly made many significant strides in treating disease, the recognition of the esoteric healing potential of flora is certainly a reminder of the interconnectedness between nature and human existence.

In this chapter, we explore the preparation of herbal remedies in the traditions of African American culture. Insight will be given into how to prepare them, utilize their therapeutic properties, and discuss the methods used to harness their healing energies.

The Wisdom of Ancestral Herbalism

Ancestral herbalism creates the space for applied concepts about body, nature, life, and spirit. The aim is to find balance and discover the truest of self within the undergird of the elements. To maintain such ideology the interpretation of African American herbalism is left to the context of circumstance. What was once seen as primitive has persevered through generations of resilience and adaptation. Oral history, family lineage, and community networks are the channels in which ancestral knowledge abides. By challenging dominant narratives of African American healing traditions, herbalists continue to honor this wisdom by forging pathways of healing using the same herbs that remain accessible today. These indigenous plants fused with ancient preparations of West African practices create a rich mosaic of herbal remedies that reflect the diverse cultural influences of the African diaspora. Drawing upon traditional recipes and techniques truly honors the sacredness of the natural world.

Herbal Tea Nourishment

Herbal tea has always been a socially shared cross-cultural delight. Made from the infusion of herbs or other plant matter, it's enjoyed daily, in cultural feasts, and ceremonious gatherings. Communal enjoyment mostly promotes calmness so that those who sip can become centered and at ease. This is perceived as preparation for the physical to receive messages from the spirit and to absorb intentional vibrations of the divine.

Knowledge of the traditional use of herbs is acquired mostly through word of mouth. It is safe to say that African American traditional remedies are simply a part of heritage. Many practitioners share the wealth of sustainable health through the careful creation of tea blends. The sensitivity of flower, root, stalk, or stem steeped in hot water stimulates the elements of living plants.

Herbal tea is not known for its quick results, but rather for its soothing nature—pun intended. In time and consistency, nature will produce dependable results. Combined with other detailed holistic practices, herbal tea uses the product of the land to rejuvenate the body from the inside out. Carefully blending berries, roots, and the leaves of plants is known to be a satisfying pleasure. The smell of fresh mint picked just as the morning dew lifts from the green of its leaves is an invigorating gift for your breakfast tea.

Tea is commonly sipped as a comforting remedy for cold and flu symptoms. It is also enjoyed daily as a sort of tonic sustaining the vitality of the organs. It's a practical method of partaking in the glory of natural wonder. Life relies upon the transformation of inorganic earth material into organic plant life. Digested, this material aids in the proper functioning of the human body.

We'll take a look at some of the traditional herbal tea blends that have served significant healing purposes for generations in the African American community; a purpose that goes well  beyond the naked eye and Western medicine prognosis. Keep in mind that curating these blends is a magickal kind of experience in which there are no true measurements of the amounts of plant essence used. However, ancestral wisdom teaches us to rely upon knowledge of the natural to guide us in our practice, as certain compounds ingested in large amounts are likely to counteract healing intentions. And so to help melodiously bring plant life together sustainably, there are a few general rules of thumb in tea preparation.

When blending use about 1/2 teaspoon of each herb in a single serving tea satchel or tea infuser. The blend and the number of herbs used in the coalesce will determine the amount to be steeped. Traditionally, one teaspoon of herb to one cup of hot water equals one serving of tea. Preparation calls for the steeping of herbs for at least 2–3 minutes. This is particular when working with flowers and leaves. With the addition of root and bark, it is advised to steep for at least 5 minutes for true potency. The longer the herbs steep, the more potent the quality of the tea.

Traditionally larger amounts or portion sizes call for 3–5 teaspoons of the herbal blend. Tea is steeped in a large glass jar in 3–5 cups of water. If not consumed hot, it was left outside in the sun or on the windowsill in full exposure for 24 to 48 hours. Nowadays the holistic way to boil water is in an enamel or nonmetallic pot.

When preparing flora to assist in healing technique, it is important to claim divine ownership over the concoction once steeped. As we become one with what we consume, even the essence of tea blends, we must also take careful consideration of the tools used to extract its ethos.

Consciousness Raising Tea

- passionflower
- lavender
- peppermint
- wormwood
- dandelion
- yarrow
- allspice (pinch)

Restfulness Tea

- dried crumbled passionflower
- honey (to taste)
  - recommended to consume 2–3 cups for effectiveness

Prophetic Dream Tea

- mint
- mullein
- mugwort
- lemon (to taste)

Healthy Womb Tea

- dried red raspberry leaf
- dried goldenrod

- dried dandelion

A Lover's Tea

- dried hibiscus leaf
- fresh ginger root (to taste)
- lemon (to taste)
- cinnamon (pinch)
- fresh orange peel shavings (pinch)

Divination Tea

- mugwort
- lemon verbena
- mint
- honey (to taste)

Anti-Inflammatory Tea

- green tea
- holy basil
- fresh ginger root
- lemon (to taste)

Ode to Strength

- comfrey
- oat straw
- nettle leaf
- calendula
- honey (to taste)

Immune Booster

- echinacea
- elderberry (actual berry)
- fresh ginger root
- 1 cinnamon stick
- honey (to taste)

Potent Herbal Tinctures

Healing and vitality can also be found in the concentrated extract of herbs, offering a potent and convenient way to wield the medicinal properties of plant life. In African American herbalism, tinctures are vibrational remedies with a few drops of aromatic essence placed directly under the tongue or in a beverage to be sipped in intervals. Traditionally used to restore balance of the emotional and mental state, it also aids in the removal of obstacles that could prevent optimum healing.

The recommended use is a four-drop dosage with your choice of liquid or by direct oral consumption, both delivering vital energy that is easily absorbed into the bloodstream. By tradition, intuition is used to select the herbs for each concoction. The most intense form of botanicals is prepared by macerating herbs with isolated intention. They can influence anything from the way the gut works to the hormonal balance of your appetite. They can also help lower blood sugar and reduce the waistline. It is said that the more bitter in taste, the better for internal organs.

Traditional blends are alcohol- or glycerin-based and are a kitchen chemistry that is a creative expression of spiritual receptivity. Ancestral wisdom does not speak of bioflavonoids, saponins, or triterpenes and how tannins give an astringent mouth feel. However, they did happen to tell lore of how tinctures were a universal antidote to any poison of the mind, body, and spirit. These blends were rarely seen due to being denied access to alcohol. Extracting their healing properties supports the immune system, relieves pain, and promotes general well-being. Ancient wisdom recognizes the personality that populates when flower essences entangle.

At the most basic level, tinctures are made with the plant or herb to be extracted, a solvent or binder, and, on occasion, a sweetener. Solvents can be alcohol (spirits), vinegar (apple cider vinegar), or even fresh honey. Herbs can be in the form of fresh leaves and stems or a dried combination of both. It is important to use the most vibrant of high-quality flora to keep the charge in the natural kinetic energy. They should be free of chemical contamination and responsibly wild-harvested as this is incorporated in the unwritten morals of practice.

Plant chemistry requires alcohol to extract flavor and preserve herbal essence long term. A few types of spirits can be used ranging from 80- to 100-proof strengths. From vodka to high-proof rums, ancestral wisdom primarily uses alcohol to call upon spiritual guidance and intention in the use of the remedy. However, apple cider vinegar and glycerin are the nonalcoholic alternatives; however, shelf life diminishes to about one year as opposed to the alcohol solvents that can last for years. There is not much detail available about how African American slaves and those before them managed to create these liquid wonders. For the sake of the lesson, we will discuss modern-day necessities that could be in the kitchen of anyone reading this book or sourced online.

Tools necessary for this method can be found in most kitchens. Items including knives, measuring cups, spoons, and mesh strainers can usually be found in the common kitchen. Other items that may need to be sourced are amber bottles, a juicer, a scale, a coffee grinder, labels, and a cast-iron pan. Of course, this is taking into account the present-day availability of these items. Herbalists of generations past may have had to be innovative and practice ingenuity using available household items to get the job done.

For the sake of historic reference to herbal candies that served as a tonic of sorts, let's presume a likely technique of African American slaves: a technique that allows one to experience the effects of bitters without the alcohol  extraction. The key is to use herbs that are not too fibrous so that it grinds well. We will explore the step-by-step breakdown of the basic processing of simple ingredients to extract herbal essence. In modern day these candies are also known as pastilles.

Materials—Herbal (Bitters) Candies

- raw honey (alcohol alternative)
- herbs
- mortar and pestle
- measuring spoon
- mixing bowl
- spoon

Technique

1. Collect herbs and honey. It is common practice to use at least one floral and one with pungent notes. Honey is the functioning sweetener and binding agent.
2. Using the mortar and pestle, grind the herbs to a thin powder. Be sure to measure the input of each herb to keep track of dosage and efficacy.
3. In a mixing bowl, combine powdered herbs with enough honey to make a thick paste (leave enough left over for dusting). The mixture should be slightly tacky, not sticky.
4. Roll paste into 1/2-inch balls.
5. End with a fresh dusting of herbs to coat the tacky quality.

Note that pastilles do not last as long as an alcohol-extracted essence, so this is a recipe meant for immediate consumption only.

We will now take a look at the technique for basic herbal tinctures. Tools suggested can be found in most common kitchens. Making tinctures is a relatively simple process and allows for greater opportunity for experimentation. Herbs and alcohol should be of the highest quality possible.

Materials—Herbal Tincture

- herb(s)—*it is recommended for the novice to start with one herb at a time.*
- knife
- cutting board
- fine mesh strainer
- mason jar
- measuring cup
- scale
- alcoholic spirit
- pen
- labels
- small brush for cleaning roots (optional)

Technique

1. Gather your herbs.
2. Dust off excess dirt from the leaves and stems. Thoroughly wash roots and clean with a small brush.
3. Being careful not to remove the bark of the root, pat dry with a paper towel or set

out into the sun to remove excess moisture.

4. Weigh the herbs then chop them finely. This will stimulate the volatility of active compounds and produce the maximum result in potency.

5. Place the herbs in a mason jar.

6. Slowly pour the spirit over the chopped herb to saturate it. Close jar tightly and shake vigorously for 30 seconds.

7. Shaking it every few days, store the tincture in a cool, dark place. Once steeped, strain into a measuring cup.

8. Bottle in amber jars to protect decoction from ultraviolet rays or light damage. Label with date, type of alcohol used, and its strength.

Crafting Protection With Herbal Salves

Historically, herbs that were the most accessible to the enslaved ancestors have been used in a plethora of ways in modern-day herbalism. The crafting of decoctions and infusions was seemingly an easier method than others. Poultices and salves were a common cross-cultural application of herbal treatment. As it was too expensive and quite rare for slaves to make tinctures using alcohol-extracting methods formulated, they made soothing ointments. Made by the infusion of the oils of herbs and combining them with beeswax, honey, or other natural emollients, these healing balms are meant for topical application only.

Herbal salves are used to soothe the skin, relieve muscle aches and pains, and promote the healing of scars or open wounds. From the nourishing minerals of sage balm to the multi-purposes of beeswax balm, salves can be considered the first kind of Vick's Vapor Rub in a sense. Modern-day African American herbalists often use salves to soothe and protect the skin as well as for other traditional uses. In preparation, herbs are selected according to their adaptogenic, immune-stimulator restorative characteristics. Infusing them in carrier oils such as olive, jojoba, avocado, chamomile, castor, or coconut oil is pertinent to extracting their highest medical benefits.

The consistency of the salve is a waterless, semi-solid mix of fatty ingredients such as wax or oil. It may contain a small amount of tincture or herbal essence. The researched definition of its significance in the lives of the first African Americans is quite vague as mostly firsthand accounts were recorded. However, through its little-known use modern-day herbalists have studied its benefits and various reasons for its application. It is prepared in a variety of forms, using an array of techniques.

Basic salve recipe variations consist of the following:

Basic Salve

- 90 milliliters of herbal-infused oil
- 10 grams beeswax

Basic Vegan Salve

- 92 milliliters of infused oil
- 8 grams of candelilla wax

Basic Herbal Remedy Salve

- 75–80 milliliters of herbal-infused oil
- 10 grams of beeswax
- 10 milliliters of herbal tincture
- 2–5 milliliters of essential oil

Basic Balm

- 67 milliliters of infused oil
- 25 grams of cacao butter—*mango and shea butter could be alternatives*
- 5 grams of beeswax
- 2 milliliters of vitamin E—*or any other carrier oil previously mentioned*
- 1 milliliter of chosen essential oil

Calendula Salve

- 3/4 cup dried calendula flowers
- 1/4 cup dried mint leaves
- 1/4 cup dried lemon balm leaves
- 1 cup of olive oil or chosen carrier oil
- 1/4 cup of beeswax
- a few drops of germanium or lavender essential oil

The generalized method of preparation starts with measuring or weighing out the wax. Depending on the choice of wax, it may need to be grated or chopped into small pieces. The herbal-infused oil or tincture is then measured out and placed with the wax in a double boiler over low heat. It is slowly whisked with a fork until visibly well-mixed and fully melted. When adding tincture, it is whisked in slowly. After fully mixed it is removed from the heat to cool off slightly. Consistency is tested with a spoon and can be returned back to the heat for adjustment. Essential oils are stirred in while the salve remains in liquid form and then immediately poured into a mason or glass jar. This is done intentionally to prevent the volatile oils from evaporating.

When adding dried leaves or flowers the process starts a bit differently. In this instance, the flowers and leaves are combined with the carrier oil. The combination is sealed in a jar tightly for 4–6 weeks in a sunny windowsill. The mixture is shaken daily, after which the infusion is strained through a cheesecloth. This is then added to the liquid form of the melted wax over low heat. Once it is well mixed, it is removed from the heat to cool off slightly before being stored in a jar or tin. Salves can be used on cuts, dry skin, and scrapes, or as needed for external healing and soothing effects.

CHAPTER 7

PURIFYING THE BODY, MIND, AND SPIRIT THROUGH SPIRITUAL BATHS AND CLEANSING RITUALS

It is crucial that practitioners have a deep understanding of the importance of spiritual baths and cleansing rituals. In the realm of African American spiritual practices, the act of cleansing holds an immense significance to the institution. Throughout the many ethnically cultural layers of history worldwide, various rituals and techniques are concentrated on purification. A multitude of rituals and techniques have been cast with this singular focus.

These rituals are emphatically intertwined with the spiritual fabric of the African American culture. They reflect not only the universal quest of cleaning the body of impurities but also the eminence of a cleansed mental and sacred physical space. From the Native American tribes to the first Africans of the Antebellum South, these ablutions are ceremonial. They incorporate Earth's elements of fire, water, essential oils, and flora, with each element chosen for its vibrational and purifying properties.

It is the underlying belief that purification rituals set the scene for individuals to not only shed physical impurities but to also rid the being of negative energies, emotional burdens, and spiritual blockages. The ultimate goal is a complete state of harmonious balance with spiritual inclination, leaving the individual in a much more malleable state of consciousness to receive messages from the divine. Across the kaleidoscope of space and time, purification rituals serve as humanity's intrinsic longing for a renewal of self, transformation of the mind, and connection to spirit. Throughout this chapter, we will continue to discuss the powerful methods of purification, such as spiritual baths and other traditional cleansing rituals.

Origins of Spiritual Baths and Cleansing Rituals

The ancient roots of spiritual baths can be traced back to civilizations across the globe. People would use the natural wonders of the sea, the river, or freshwater springs to partake in physical and spiritual cleansing. From the sacred rivers of India to the traditional sweat lodges of Native American tribes, cleansing practices have been a part of spiritual traditions for millennia. Religion holds water sacred for baptism, a symbol of transition into a higher spiritual self. It can also be interpreted as a spiritual rite of passage. It was customary for some cultures to use spiritual bathing as a social therapeutic experience of purification.

Ancient African rituals used the art of spiritual baths as part of the art of herbal medicine. Baths were used to treat skin disorders, respiratory conditions, genital diseases, and spiritual ailments. Rituals would typically be accompanied by a prayer or affirmation of spiritual influence. African ancestral rituals were not allowed to be observed in active practice as the possible presence of idle energies could invite tribulation, as well as cloud the spiritual pathways to receiving messages.

In many cultures, flora played a prominent role in cleansing rituals. Specific plants chosen for their purification properties were believed to possess powers that were capable of warding off evil spirits. The power of water, specifically after it was blessed with intention, was a direct line to internal salvation. To be revered as not only essential for life of the physical but also a metaphor for one to submerge themselves into the depths of consciousness to find the most balanced self.

Significance of Spiritual Baths and Cleansing Rituals in African American Herbalism

Spiritual baths and cleansing rituals hold profound significance in the spiritual and magickal modalities of African American herbalism. At their core, these practices are for the expiation of psychic debris, removing stagnant energies while cleansing energetic bodies and negative emotions that have accumulated over time. Spirituality is expressed in context of the cleansing practice. This supports the sentiment that these rituals were used especially for individuals to spiritually ascend during times of crisis.

Particularly significant in individual experiences, spiritual baths are capable of transforming one from a distressed state to an enhanced sense of well-being. Cleansing rituals help to acknowledge pain and are catalytic vessels for spiritual connectedness. Culturally used to restore positive family dynamics and to protect children from danger or individuals from misfortunes, ancestral wisdom teaches modern-day herbalists and spiritual healers to use cleansing rituals in daily practice. Descendants of spiritual healers have been taught that blended herbal baths used with divinations can cure disharmony within the community as well as bring clarity or solace in moral disorder.

As powerful tools for intention setting, spiritual baths and cleansing rituals are key to manifestation. By blessing a body of water and infusing it with specific herbs, essential oils, or even crystals, the scene is set for commencing with focused intention. This process is a transformative one: It empowers the practitioner to release the things that no longer serve them and to embrace the fresh breath of new beginnings, all with revealed clarity and purpose.

Preparing for Spiritual Baths or Cleansing Rituals

Detoxifying the body and spirit requires a little bit of preparation. Traditionally herbal baths and rituals are quite elaborate setups. First, a sacred space must be created and made conducive to meditative reflection and energetic purification. Preparations may involve the burning of incense, the blessing of divination tools, and even the use of mud.

Accompanied by spiritual sayings and libations, baths can be prepped by male or female herbalists and spiritual healers. It is recorded that in ancient times preparation was left to the wise elders of communities. They would make the baths in big earthen or wooden bowls. Baths were often prepared in front yards and poured onto the head of the individual with a calabash. Leaves were left on the body to permeate the skin with healing properties.

Herbalists today begin cleansing the chosen sacred space with sacred herbs such as dried white sage, palo santo (cedar wood stick), or sweetgrass. This disperses any stagnant energy while inviting positive, healing vibrations. The lighting of candles, the burning of incense, and high vibrational music further enhance the atmosphere for the commencement of the ritual.

Next, the necessary preparation of ingredients is an intuitive notion. Herbs, essential oils, salt, and crystals are gathered relative to the intention or desired outcome.

Novice practitioners should consult master herbalists or masterful spiritual guides to choose the most suitable ingredient. Additionally, the placement of ritual tools or sacred objects that hold personal significance are used to uniquely dress the purified space.

Creating the Sacred Bath

After all ingredients have been gathered and the space is blessed with purified intention, the time is right to draw the bath. The tub of personal choice is filled with warm water. The temperature is meant to be comfortable for immersion. As the bath fills, it is infused with essential oils, herbs, crystals, and intentions. Visualizing the desired outcome is key when imbuing the bath with vibrational healing essence.

As the bath is prepared, clear intention attracts an abundance of healing energy. Once the individual is immersed it will release the negative and cultivate an inner peace. Intention must be articulated with conviction and a clear, open mind. The immersed individual is instructed to envision the healing waters revitalizing their being and washing away the impurities of the mind, body, and spirit.

Conducting the Cleansing Ritual

At this point, intention is clear and set in both the practitioner and client. The client is instructed to let the high vibrations of the infused water swathe them. Practitioner and client must center themselves with a few deep breaths, being consciously aware of the present moment and remaining connected to the elements used in the ritual. Those in attendance are left to embrace the purifying energies as the client feels the rejuvenation from a cellular level, washing away impurities and negativity.

As the client soaks in healing essence, it is requisite to the practice for one to engage in mindful meditation, chant, visualization, or prayer. The client is expected to reflect on any emotions, thoughts, or sensations that present themselves during the ritual. They are coached to surrender to the healing process in its entirety. Guided with the wisdom of intuition, the client will find transformative insight in the mindfulness of requisite.

Within several minutes of immersion, the client is guided to imagine any remaining negativity or energetic blockages dissolving into the water. Deep breaths of renewal and purification should follow. When ready, the client will gently emerge from the bath to be pat dry with a clean, white towel. It is important that consciousness stays enthralled in the sacredness of the moment. A cardinal point is that gratitude must be expressed for the gift of intention and the healing of ritual bestowed upon practitioners.

In the diverse striations of African American cleansing practices, some cleansing rituals call for the client or practitioner to partake in a series of baths, according to the severity of the cleansing. Each bath constitutes a step in the healing process or designed treatment of affliction. Each is meant to shed layers of negativity or anything blocking the free movement of love, light, and peace.

It is said that adding frankincense as the essential oil of choice will open the crown chakra, eliminating confusion and depression.

Alternatively, a small round disk of charcoal is placed in a cast-iron or fireproof bowl. The charcoal is lit and, when burning red hot, a few crumbled rocks of frankincense is sprinkled on top of it to burn. It is usually placed on a trivet to avoid burning the floor, table, or other standing structure.

By engaging in these sacred practices with intention and reverence, individuals have a safe space to cleanse themselves of accumulated impurities of the mind, body, and spirit. It is a chance to embody the pure light of love of self and divine purpose: a chance to transcend to the spiritual realm and dive deeper into the energetic layers of the spiritual self. It is a sacred trek to confronting and releasing energies that no longer serve the greater good of the life of the individual.

Spiritual cleansing invites the practitioner to tap into the wellspring of unconditional love and divine wisdom from within—a plausible route to eradicate self-doubt, fear, and spiritual 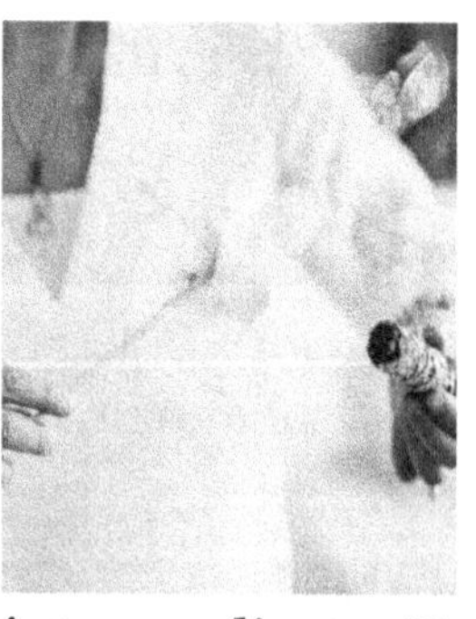 opposition that obscures one's true radiance. To cleanse spiritually is to allow the brilliance of the soul to shine with an impetuous brightness. It is a reclamation of one's inherent worth and affirms that the human body is a vessel of divine energy and infinite potential. It forces self-compassion and acceptance for the divine to spark that which dwells within.

Furthermore, this practice offers a gateway to aligning one with a divine purpose and a higher calling. Individuals are called to attune to the whispers of spirit and remain open to the guidance the universe brings through the use of the elements:

- Burning jasmine incense will help to set balance and bring forth peace.
- Sage smudging with the windows open will provide an exit for the released negative energies.
- A bath with lavender oil will support a keen intuition, concentration on peace of mind, and creating inner space for clarity.
- Eucalyptus promotes successful communication and compassion with divine love while also healing all energy blocks of the throat area.
- The use of bergamot oil will increase divination with uplifting mental alertness. It stimulates an astute relief of

anxiety, depression, grief, and sadness while helping to strengthen the immune system. It also serves as an antiseptic, healing wounds and scars.

- Rose oil helps to release intimacy blockage and helps to eliminate circulation problems, heart problems, repressed love, and emotional instability.

Essentially, spiritual cleansing rituals offer the individual a chance to feed their spirit in a space meant for the transformative journey of self-love, empowerment, and spiritual awakening. It's a sacred proverbial dance of release, renewal, and purification wherein practitioners have the opportunity to emerge from the spiritual bath with newfound radiance and a divine understanding of life's purpose. This cleansing ritual is a profound act of self-care and spiritual devotion. It is the affinity to manipulate the elements to be able to embody the pure light of love and spiritual healing. Practitioners learn how to better diffuse their essence out into the world after partaking in these practices. African American herbalism and magick compel practitioners, spiritual healers, and master herbalists to remain open to ongoing self-discovery.

CHAPTER 8

ANCESTRAL RITUALS AND BEHAVIORS

Ceremonious tradition can be an expression of celebration, mourning, rite of passage, or simply the glory of spiritual growth. Ceremony is a time to honor life, love, and community. Rituals and ancestral ceremonies were designed to facilitate communal healing, protection, prosperity, and interconnectedness with the ancestors. Drawing from ancient wisdom, these practices are a fixture in the African American communities. They are vibrant, elaborate, usually festive occasions that are blended with ancient African traditions as well as modern magickal practices.

Ancient Ritual History and Tradition

Historically, enslaved people were prohibited from performing traditional ritualistic acts. They were severely reprimanded for practicing spiritual works and punished while accused of conspiring to rebel against authority. Enslaved Africans were held responsible for preparing the bodies of the deceased, including the loved ones of the plantation owner. However, because of the disallowance of ancient tradition, funerals were held in hidden sacred spaces called hush harbors. These spaces were created by the enslaved for the people in systematic bondage to freely honor the Earthly passing as well as the transition spirit and to perform funeral rituals without negative repercussions.

Traditions were maintained in subtle ways and carried over into the complex legacies of the Western world. These traditions evolved with the variance of Caribbean and Native American influences yet share a range of similar foundational qualities. One quality is the acknowledgment of a supreme being and another major quality is the belief that spirit lives within everything.

Ancestral traditions involved polyrhythmic dancing, spiritual songs, call-and-response chants, and sacred music. Often times in veneration of the ancestors, circle dancing with water immersion and divination practice used spiritual charms to invoke protection against harmful encounters during rituals. Some ancestral ceremonies summoned the elders of the community to pour spirits, libations, or holy water in each cardinal direction. This was to honor the recently passed ancestors right before a couple sought guidance to be wed.

Wedding Rituals

Jumping the broom was also a wedding ritual dating back to Africa and the transatlantic slave trade, although research finds it as a Welsh, Celtic tradition dating back to Roma cultural practices. Since the enslaved were seen as comparable to cattle in the eyes of plantation owners, their desire to marry was not recognized by the government agency. Instead, the broom was used ceremoniously as a metaphor to signify a new beginning, sweeping away the past, validating the union, and offering respect to the ancestors for their blessing. These non-church weddings provided one of many unique cultural diffusions in ancestral rituals. Regardless of the denunciation of the marriage of slaves, the communities endorsed the marriage, recognizing the moral and spiritual union of kindred souls.

The Power of Music

Rituals offering prayer, food, and dance filled with spirit help to tell the stories of survival. They help to build the spiritual resistance of a people and keep the culture alive for generations to observe. Bush meetings, as ancestral African American ceremonial gatherings were sometimes referred to, were spaces where spirits were known to take over the body. These gatherings were praise houses of dance, chant, and ring shout, a shuffling, circular dance. Hand clapping and euphoric trance animated the intention to gather. An African-American-relative term, spirituals, is derived from songs that were sung during the rituals and ceremonies of slaves. During ceremonious rituals, song has a way of expressing hope and sorrow, as well as their parallels in spirituality. Music was and still is a vessel for communication. It is a  correspondent to the spirit realm and melodic composition of expression or release of emotions using the traditions of rituals.

Music acts as a bridge between the physical and the ethereal, the seen and the unseen. Across cultures and throughout recorded African American history, music has been esteemed as a sacred art form capable of transcending linguistic barriers. It is a virtuous collection of sounds that seem to communicate directly to the soul of practitioners partaking in ritual. Whether it is the rhythmic beating of drums or the hoisting of spirit through song, music infuses spiritual gatherings with vibrational resonance that reverberates in the deepest nooks of the human psyche. Melodic composition allows practitioners to elicit a wide range of emotional intensities, conveying anything from joy and enchantment to grief and hopelessness. It's the recurrent nature of the melody that allows practitioners to take a journey inward to explore their spiritual essence and connect with the divine. There is even light in the silence that breaks the internal barriers of darkness. In this sacred space of sonic alchemy, music becomes an influential channel for ritual as it is still used for interaction with spirit, transformative healing, and spiritual awakening.

Symbolic Acts

Definitively, ritualistic practice could be viewed as a system of symbolic acts that are based upon arbitrary rules. However, its significance goes beyond mere arbitrary action. Modern-day African American herbalists use the art of ritualistic practices to embody deeply held beliefs, values, and intentions within a spiritual context. While the specific actions and spiritual guidelines may appear whimsical from a novice or outsider's perspective, they in fact hold great meaning and significance in the framework of African American tradition.

These symbolic acts serve to sanctify the sacred space, marking transitions into spiritual enlightenment and inviting divine presence while facilitating collective and individual transformation of the mind. Ancestral wisdom teaches that practitioners who are able to tap into the collective consciousness through ritual can also connect with the natural to access hidden spiritual depths of insightful healing. While rituals may seemingly be embedded with arbitrary rules, the power of the act of ceremony in the African American culture lies within the inevitable faculty to profoundly shift one's frame of mind, consciousness, and state of internal balance.

In this chapter we shall continue to probe the menagerie ritualistic ascent and steps to prepare for ceremonies that draw from the ancient wisdom of African American traditions, as well as from the magick of modern modalities. These rituals require practitioners to possess a wealth of knowledge about natural law and human connection. Masterful herbalists combine their affinity to flora with the potency of technique and intention to create powerful sacred places for members of the community to unite to explore collective transformation in all parts of life; convening whether to seek emotional, physical, or spiritual guidance, cleansing, and holistic daily routes to healing. Rituals can safeguard against negative energy, help honor the wisdom of the ancestors, and invite an abundance of prosperity into the lives of practitioners.

Ritual Behaviors and Observances

Rituals can be positive or negative, as a negative act's connotation is an avoidance of behavior in relation to the positive. In other words, every action has a positive or negative reaction. Design of ritual action truly depends on the belief system of the community and explicit intention. Ritual behavior has been established from ancestral wisdom and observed traditions. It is a profound aspect of human culture and African American spirituality that has been passed down from one generation to the next. It is a lineage of knowledge serving as testament to the perpetual power of rituals, reminding us to connect with something greater than ourselves, albeit a connection to the divine, the natural world, or spirits that guide us. A universalized fact at the core of rituals, irrespective of cultural and spiritual backgrounds, is that ritual begins with making an altar: a foundational act that goes beyond the act of physically building or constructing a sacred spiritual space. It is one symbolic of the manifestation of intention, divine communication, and divine purpose through rituals.

The making of an altar is a thoughtful and deliberate process, allowing one to reflect on circumstance with gratitude and inviting communal sharing of spiritual beliefs, intentions, and healing desires. It is a quiet place in a corner of your home, serving as a focal point for spiritual energy. It is a space for communion with spirit and ancestral guides, a container for symbolic objects, and sacred symbols that represent significant power. Adorning the altar with meaningful trinkets, symbolic figurines, and offerings will propel the intentions of your spiritual practice. These objects should include a representation of the natural elements, drawing from the healing energies of stones, plants, or water.

1. Begin by selecting cloth (as discussed in previous chapters) or an altar runner in a color that propagates your intentions. For example, green for prosperity and purple for spiritual connection.
2. Next, arrange crystals, figurines, and other sacred items that hold personal significance, infusing the space with vibrational objects. Nature's beauty should be incorporated, such as fresh flowers, herbs, sand, or fresh grass, to further increase vibrational frequency and remain connected to the natural world.
3. After carefully arranging artifacts and symbolic figures on the altar, be sure to give gratitude for the support of the natural.

Creating the altar is a ritualistic gesture that signifies readiness and respect for the light of the universe in ritual. It is a mental and spiritual preparation that creates a harmonized internal and physical space primed for the ritual's success. Practitioners are able to express their commitment and reverence for tradition while creating an altar. It is a chance to be grounded in the glory of ancestral wisdom and accumulated knowledge. Consider the altar as the focal point for the ritual's energies, where the metaphysical and the natural world collide in adjunction. It is where communications with the spirit world are transmitted, enabling a flow of energy that brings forth the intentions of the practitioner. Finally, the altar should be consecrated with a spiritual prayer or smoke blessing, to beseech divine presence to bless the sacred space.

Healing Bath Rituals

Ritual is a form of nonverbal communication during a sacred time, in a sacred place. As we have explored earlier, one of the most plausible ways to employ the healing energies of plant life is  through herbal infusion in ritual baths or as aromatic therapy during rituals. A blend of herbs is chosen because of their healing properties. Chosen herbs are assembled and placed into a clean, heat-tolerant vessel, such as a glass jar. Boiling water is then poured over the herbs to steep for at least 5–7 minutes in order to extract their essence. As preparation for the infusion commences, healing intentions are to be imbued by visualization of the herbs working in synergy to restore balance of the mind, body, and spirit. Once the infusion has steeped for several minutes, the herbs are strained and dispensed into a diffuser, teacup, or directly into a warm bath.

Step-By-Step Herbal Bath Preparations

1. Prepare space

    A.   Cleanse the area with sage or palo santo.

    B.   Set up divination tools and symbols that resonate with healing energy.

2. Gather ingredients

    A.   Choose herbal selections.

    B.   Optional: Add Epsom salt or sea salt to intensify vibrational frequencies and promote relaxation.

3. Prepare bath

    A.   Fill bath with warm water.

    B.   Add herbal selection and salts to infuse water with healing energies.

    C.   Set your intentions

4. Visualize the water being charged with healing light while stirring clockwise with your hand.

    A.   Close your eyes and pay close attention to your breath.

B.   Taking several deep breaths, visualize the water enveloping you with healing energies. Imagine all discomforts soothed and washed away by the bath infusion.

C.   State your intentions for the healing bath and steer focus toward your desired outcome.

5.   Bathing with intention

A.   Slowly immerse yourself in the healing waters, taking the time to express gratitude to the elements that contribute to your healing experience.

B.   Visualize any pain or tension washing away and replaced with a sense of balance within a peaceful well-being.

C.   Spend about 30 minutes soaking up the healing vibrations.

6.   Express gratitude

A.   When you are ready to exit the bath, be sure to thank the natural elements for their healing energies as remnants of plant essence permeate the skin.

B.   Pat dry with a clean white towel. A feeling of rejuvenation should fill your being at this point.

Step-By-Step   Forest   Bathing—Using Sound

1. Find your favorite space in the woods or forest.
2. Take a seat with your back resting against the tree.
3. Begin deep belly breaths or fire breaths.
4. Focused on your breathing and let the mind settle, allowing the sounds of the forest to fill the space between the breath and the exhale.
5. Notice the sensation upon touching the tree, the smells, the air, and the feel of the earth beneath you.

6. Place your hand on your heart and sing something from the soul. If that doesn't suit you, try taking the time to release and simply scream.
7. Afterward, rise and hug the tree, thanking it for its remedy upon departure.

Step-By-Step Grief Releasing Bath

1. Bring a large pot of water to a boil.
2. Place a handful of chosen herbs into the pot.
3. Cover. Let contents steep for up to 3 hours, no less than 45 minutes.
4. This bath works best when drawn in correlation with moon energies. In correlation, steeping should be overnight in the light of the full moon for supreme release of energies.
5. Strain the herbs.
6. Add a few splashes of Florida water with 8 ounces of coconut milk.
7. Pour the mixture into your bath and let the power of the plants wash over you as you soak.

Step-By-Step Personal Trauma Healing Bath

1. Pray over a large pot filled with fresh spring water. Ask the divine for the desired outcome.

2. Add a handful of black walnuts to the water and bring to a boil.
3. Turn off the heat and add associated plants and flowers, as well as a couple splashes of Florida water.
4. Cover. Steep for at least an hour.

   A. Steep overnight in the moonlight.

5. Add a small amount of fresh earth or natural clay.
6. Place crystals (black tourmaline and rose quartz) into the pot.
7. Strain out the plant material. Pour liquid into bath water or over yourself in the shower.

Step-By-Step Healing the Body Temple Bath

1. Prepare your spiritual wash.

   A. Use cold or room temperature purified water—or 1 quart of rainwater.

   B. Add a drop of honey and a handful of hyssop leaves.

   C. Let steep.

D. Maybe use a muslin bag or nylon stocking instead of a free pour of herbs.

2. Cover all the mirrors in the bathroom.
3. Burn incense.

A. Traditionally frankincense and myrrh, though modern-day Nag Champa and Dragon's Blood will work.

4. Give yourself a scrub in the tub using African black soap, or a natural coconut oil-based soap.

A. Use warm water to wash downward in prayer and song.

5. Pour the spiritual wash over your head and allow it to run down, washing your temple.

A. Listen to the spirit within and repeat this step as many times as needed until the higher self feels renewed and lifted from any blockage.

These baths help to clear personal spiritual paths while casting fear, illness, or negativity from one's life. Ritual allows one to release, renew, and reenergize one's energy, giving practitioners a safe place to entertain spiritual  balance as well as a soul-stirring personal experience with the truths of the divine.

Protection With Sacred Stones or Crystals

Stone grids are a powerful tool for amplifying intention and creating energetic protection in your home or sacred space. The ritual begins with the selection of sacred bones of Earth, which are the stones, crystals, and gems found in the wondrous bounty of the heartbeat of Earth. Chosen according to their protective properties, ancestral lore speaks of the semiprecious stones or gems worn by the people of the ancient Nile Valley. Ancestral wisdom teaches that the same precious stones worn thousands of years ago have the same power as spiritual protectors today. Each stone channels a certain type of energy and works closely with the human chakras to open them up for energy stimulation. Stones were also worn as sacred jewelry for rituals, auric cleansings, and room energy activators.

Commonly used modern-day examples of sacred stones are black tourmaline for grounding, jade for the generation of divine love, amethyst for dispelling anger, controlling emotional temperament, eliminating pain, or providing the individual with dignity, and clear quartz for amplification of intentions or vibrational frequencies from spirit. It is important that a quiet space is found where you can lay out your chosen crystals in a geometric pattern, such as a circle or triangle. While arranging and organizing your sacred stones, focus on intentions for protection.

As you cultivate your sacred space, focus on the radiance of energetic light surrounding it. Envision it as a luminous barrier for your personal sanctuary. This light is a powerful force field, emanating from the core of your being and extending outward to encompass protective intentions. Visualize radiant energies as shimmering protective veils that are impenetrable shields against any intrusion of your sanctuary or sacred space. Intentional points of convergence lie in the repelling of any form of negative thoughts, energies, or influences. Energies of your sacred space coalesce with each breath, affirming the influence of your stones. Attuning yourself to the frequencies of the grid frees the mind from intrusive thoughts or burdens.

Once you have infused your surroundings with the transformative energy of divine grace and the grid is complete, activate it by tracing a line of mugwort (or any herb to facilitate divination) from stone to stone. This act will connect them in a unified field of protection. Then place a candle or sacred item of significance in the center of the grid to anchor its energies. With unwavering focus, set your sights on the intentional point of convergence. The key is to keep it charged with protective vibrations and maintain the integrity of its sacred existence.

Prosperity Ritual With Herbal Sachets

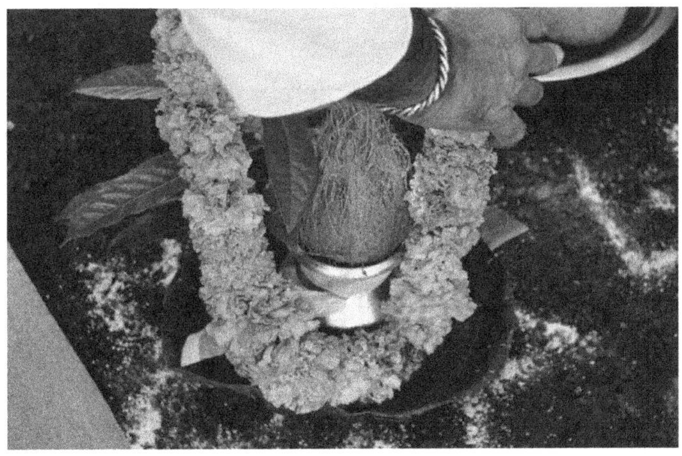

Traditionally sachet bags can be made out of any type of comely fabric. Lace, satin, silk, cotton, and muslin are apropos for divination work. Think of this special bag as a sacred item that holds your spirit. These bags are meant to be small and likely fragrant. They are a simple, dynamic way to infuse your home or workspace with the energies of abundance and prosperity.

For your first sachet, begin by selecting herbs according to their energetic properties. For prosperity, we'll use lavender and calendula as examples for this practice. First, collect a small bunch of lavender flowers and lay them out in a single layer to dry. Note that dried lavender and calendula flowers are very accessible in modern day. However, if you have the simple pleasure of finding these aromatic jewels just outside your door, connect with the elements and dry the flowers yourself.

After they are completely dry, grind them finely with a mortar and pestle. A blender or a food processor will also work just fine, though most rely on the sacred old-fashioned way of using the mortar and pestle as it keeps the sanctity of ancestral sacred items pure. Once grounded finely, fill the cloth bag and seal or sew up the openings. When using more than one herb, allow the bag some time to age and give the herbs some time to fuse. At some point, try adding citrus peels and spices to the crushed flowers as it will enhance the intention put forth into the mixture. Once the sachet is ready, place it in a prominent location in the chosen environment. It could be placed above the entrance of your home, the drawers of your desk, or the inside of pillowcases and cushions. Place them where they can radiate energetic influence and attract prosperity. It is necessary to refresh the herbs every so often to keep the essence of the sachet vibrant and abundant.

Step-By-Step Abundance Bath

1. Bring a large pot of hot water to a boil.
2. Turn off the burner. Place a handful of lavender and calendula (or your own combination of herbs) into the pot. Cover.

   A. Let it sit for 45 minutes.
   B. If using the phases of the moon or the energy of the sun, allow it to sit overnight under the moonlight or steep under the sun on an exposed windowsill.

3. Strain.

4. Add 3 splashes of Florida water or coconut milk before slowly dispensing it in a drawn bath.

    A. For increased effects, add a citrine crystal with 8 ounces of coconut milk and 1/4 cup of honey.

    B. If using a shower, pour it over your head in three-sequence pours as you focus on the abundance flowing into your life.

5. Remain in the essence of the bath. Do not rinse it off.

    A. Be sure to cover your head if you must go out into public.

Sacred (Ancestral) Medicine Bag

- sage (leaf or essential oil)
- crystals or precious stones
- frankincense and myrrh
- incense burner
- rejuvenation herbal extract
- aloe vera gel
- purification or spiritual prayer, chant, or song

Incorporating rituals into everyday life can enrich your spiritual practice with the guidance of ancestral wisdom. Rituals are a pathway to protection, prosperity, and ancestral connection.  They invite us to tap into magickal energies influenced by the natural world while finding alignment with our highest potential. Harnessing the wisdom of the natural, herbs, crystals, and sacred baths can amplify your intentions and achieve clarity through practice.

Whether creating a sacred space or altar, crafting herbal decoctions, or cleansing the aura of negative energies, each ritual or ceremonious act is an opportunity to deepen spiritual practice, presenting a chance to cultivate internal harmony, while bringing forth abundance and existential balance. Embracing the magick of African American tradition is a journey of self-discovery and a transformative initiative to the infinite possibilities of your sacred path.

CHAPTER 9
COMMUNITY AND HEALING

Herbalism has allowed the profound narrative of the resilience of a people to underscore techniques for survival, healing, and transformation. These people were stolen from their country and sold into slavery in Europe, the West Indies, and the Americas. To add insult to injury they were subjected to the worst kind of violence that one human can perpetrate on another. Amidst the historical circumstances and ongoing trauma, the community has cultivated generations of unique healing modalities, all grounded in the ancestral wisdom of herbalism and the power of magick. As a people that still carry the scars of generations of unethical inhumanities, deep hurt of the soul has been passed down from generation to generation. Ancestral practices have provided a communal pathway to physical and emotional healing. It has played a crucial role in fostering strength within the community and a deep sense of belonging and identity.

Historical Context and the Roots of Herbalism and Magick

The transatlantic slave trade left an inedible mark on the African continent and diaspora. Considered one of the most heinous and devastating realities of world history, it commenced at the start of the 15th century and continued for over 400 years. This brutal system of commerce forcefully displaced millions of families of African descent or nationality, separating mother from daughter, father from son, and husband from wife to subject them to unimaginable suffering, generations of exploitation, and daily dehumanization. The impact of the transatlantic slave trade on cultural identity and the dislocation and adaptation of it cannot be overstated. It was a system that severed individuals from their roots, and even caused mothers to kill their own children as a form of protection from abuse. It fractured familial and community ties while upending century-old traditions and belief systems.

Despite these harrowing circumstances, the diaspora has found ways to preserve their cultural practices as the enslaved forged spiritual expression from adaptation within the confinement of plantation life. Herbalism and magick served as a lifeline for the enslaved, offering a safe space of solace, healing, and resistance within the substance of community against the dehumanizing forces of slavery. Drawing upon diverse ancient spiritual traditions, including those of West Africa, Central Africa, and the Caribbean Islands, enslaved individuals engaging in clandestine rituals or ceremonies were provided a connection to their spiritual guides or ancestors. This served and still serves as a source of hope: a sense of prideful empowerment and a means to resist their oppressors.

The transatlantic slave trade profoundly shaped the cultural landscape of the African American diaspora. A variety of traditions, beliefs, and practices reflect how sacred practices were essential to resistance and survival, as well as the indomitable spirit of those who endured unimaginable hardships. The legacy of cultural adaptation and survival endures the legacies of systemic oppression and racism.

Herbalism in the African American Community

The art of herbalism within the African American community is indicative of a true adaptability in spite of circumstance. Master herbalists, root doctors, or simply herbal  healers have historically been important figures of the community, offering remedies and guidance in times of need to those who sought their help. These healers, often times women, have wielded ancestral knowledge of local flora, using plants like yarrow root for healing and dressing wounds or spearmint for reinvigorating stress relief, and elderberry for its antiviral properties.

Serving as pillars of the community, holistic healers hold a position of respect and authority in being the source of wisdom in times of need. Their affinity to the plant world and deep understanding of the medicinal uses of plants give credence to their communal position. Their understanding is passed down through generations of oral tradition and practical experience, encompassing not only the physical healing properties of herbs but also the spiritual and metaphysical significance.

They serve as mediators between the forces of the natural and spiritual realms. Mediation is in the herbal remedies and guidance sought out for a wide range of ailments. With a keen sense of intuition and an interconnectedness with the elements and their health-promoting properties, healers are able to tailor specific treatments to address particular concerns, needs, and circumstances of the client or individual. They live by the holistic principle that healing is all-encompassing, as it is not of the body only but also mind and spirit.

In addition to their roles as healers, masterful herbalists are educators, protectors, and guardians of cultural heritage within the African American community. Here is just a snippet of what they do:

- passing down their knowledge to the next generation and ensuring the continuity of healing traditions and ancient healing practices
- offering apprenticeships, workshops, personal consultations, and community gatherings to impart the technical skills of herbalism and uphold the spiritual

principles and the ethical values that underpin work with the divine

- offering insight as spiritual guides and advisors as their connection to the natural world and unseen realms gives them the ability to perceive or interpret messages from the spirit
- providing clarity to those facing challenges or uncertainties in their immediate day-to-day life

During times of crisis, whether by natural forces or periods of heightened racial tension, spiritual healers are called upon to provide the service of comfort and guidance to their communities. Through rituals and herbal remedies, they offer solace and instill hope in the face of adversity. These guardians of cultural heritage are stewards of spiritual and natural wisdom. Their contributions to the African American diaspora are invaluable, past, present, and future. Contributions often encompass spiritual and emotional proportions, reinforcing the reciprocity of well-being in the community.

Magick and Spirituality

The practice of magick represents a powerful means of navigating a world marked by marginalization. These traditional practices empower individuals and communities alike. This book is a testament to African American magick's spiritual influence across belief systems within the American context. Through ritual, practitioners engage with the spiritual realm, seeking guidance through turmoil, solace in the unexplained, and protection from imperilment. This spiritual engagement fosters a sense of agency, grounding individuals in a recognizable cultural identity.

As a sacred conduit connecting divine forces, ancestral spirits, and unseen vibrations, using magick to help heal the collective is rooted in ancestral wisdom. Strengthening protective factors increases resilience and facilitates spiritual engagement so that liberation can be attained in the highest morality. The magick in African American spirituality is the construct of relationships and the social support that comes with communal rituals. Whether through prayer, meditation, ceremony, or spiritual cleansing, individuals call upon the spirit and the ancestors with unified intentions.

Magick and spirituality affirm a connection to lineage and psychologically enhance the state of the community. Positively supporting a gracious relationship with the divine, cultural connection is on the path of discovery in traditional acts. Spirituality requires practice to cope with life's transgressions and is seen as the ultimate tool in finding meaning as well as purpose in the lessons. Unexplained phenomena somehow make sense of the inexplicable and offer comfort in the midst of chaos. Lore and ritualistic practices give individuals the chance to reclaim their heritage and assert sovereignty in the face of affliction. In acts of devotion, reverence, and spiritual observance, inspiration is drawn from collective wisdom and the experiences of the ancestors.

By warding off malevolent forces that may threaten the safety of the members of the community, ritualistic magick remains a powerful resource. Energy expelled through charms, crystals, or any other divine object stirs the energetic forces of spiritual guides, especially with the mass intention set forth. A shield of divine protection is reinforced in a group setting. This can be described as proactive engagement that instills a sense of fortitude while confronting adversity with courage and determination.

Healing From Collective Trauma

What is collective trauma? Collective trauma is the psychological distress of a group of people derived from a catastrophic event that affects their collective identity and sense of security, creating communal imbalances. Unlike individual traumas, collective trauma leaves deep, lasting scars on the collective psyche. In the widespread adversity, suffering, loss, displacement, and disruption of social cohesion, a shared sense of vulnerability and existential threat also has a way of bringing people together.

A defining characteristic of collective trauma is its intergenerational transmission of psychological effects through successive generations, occurring through various mechanisms, including familial narratives, cultural norms, and societal structures. The trauma is embedded in the collective memory of a people, shaping their beliefs and behaviors over time.

Collective trauma manifests a variety of physical, emotional, and social symptoms that impact the community on multiple levels. These levels host feelings of fear, anxiety, depression, anger, and grief, as well as post-traumatic stress disorder. It disrupts social relationships, erodes trust in institutions, and exacerbates existing inequalities and injustices within the diaspora.

Healing from collective trauma requires a multifaceted approach that addresses all of the above, including cultural capacities. This could involve individual, family, or group therapy, community-based initiatives, psychoeducation, and advocacy for systemic change. Cultural practices such as storytelling and cleansing baths play a crucial role in the acknowledgment and processing of said trauma. Complex and pervasive, it continues to impact an entire sect of people.

However, in recent years there has been a resurgence of interest in the communal wonders of ritual. This resurgence is fueled by a desire for community and reconnection in a  fragmented group and within an individualistic society. In a world marked by social isolation, digital communications, and marginalization, many still long for a sense of belonging and acceptance. They look to be a part of something greater in the physical realm, driven by a growing awareness of the social crises facing humanity.

Healing circles or gatherings like wellness events or African American celebrations provide a safe space to share stories. It's an opportunity to support others who share the same healing path and journey. As people grapple with social inequality, it makes it a tad bit more bearable when there is a general feeling of understanding bestowed by the community.

Rituals centered around stewardship and social justice bring the community together to address pressing challenges and intentionally envision a more just future. Community gardens allow members to reconnect with the healing powers of the land in a shared space of solidarity. By embracing the wisdom of ancient traditions and harnessing the energies of communal ritual, social change transcends historic limitations. By grounding efforts in shared values and spiritual principles, the African American community mobilizes collective energies to tackle inequities and promote cultural sustainability.

Juneteenth, now recognized as a federal holiday, is a poignant example of ritualistic gatherings or celebrations that bring people together to heal in reverence. On June 19th, 1865, nearly two years after the Emancipation Proclamation, Texas finally broke news to the enslaved that they were actually free. This date became known as Juneteenth, or Freedom Day. The proclamation stated that all men were free and gave absolute equality of rights between slaves and the plantation owners. A resting oppression lives within these facts themselves. In triumph, Juneteenth is a reflection on the legacy of slavery and its long-lasting impact on society. To celebrate freedom collectively, the African American community continues to reaffirm their commitment to honoring the experiences of the ancestors, seeking justice, and generational healing. Celebrations include panel discussions, workshops, dance performances, music, tons of food, storytelling, and family fun encouraging togetherness in communal engagement. It is a collective honoring of the past and the highly restricted lives of those who no longer inhabit this realm.

Similarly, ritualistic gatherings centered around social injustices can be a vessel for ongoing healing in the form of peace vigils or cultural awareness rallies. These gatherings bring people together in solidarity to inherently find healing of collective wounds and to envision a more equitable future. Building bridges of understanding across the barriers of racial and cultural divides. Weaving the values of stewardship, justice, and empathy into communal fabrics of healing helps to bring about a shared purpose that can propel communal intentions.

Herbalism and magick serve as both a link to the resilient ancestors and a tool for addressing generational struggles, transforming pain into empowerment and grief into collective strength.

A Sense of Belonging in Resistance

The reclamation and practice of herbalism

and magick within the African American diaspora are acts of cultural preservation and resistance. As the human spirit holds an innate capacity to agitate against injustices, it also craves liberation. However, resistance is no mere feat and is not a solitary endeavor: It thrives in the context of magick within community, where struggles meet in synchronized hopes and intentions. Through a multidimensional lens, let us delve into the intersection of spirituality, resistance, and the effects of an actively healing community. Let's continue to explore the illuminating, transformative effects of practices that nurture resilience, healing, and liberation.

Understanding Belonging in Resistance

Belonging in resistance is about finding a home within the proverbial walls of a cultural community. A community, in this sense, is a group of like-minded individuals who share common visions of justice and equality for a people. They share a deep sense of connection that transcends individual differences and brings people to a common ground against the confinements of oppression culturally. Ironically belonging in resistance provides a sanctuary of sorts. It is a place where historically silenced individuals can be seen, heard, and valued as human beings—valued for who they are and what they stand for. It is both a sanctuary where they can find strength and support and a place where they can collectively imagine and visualize virtue.

Spirituality, with its emphatic focus on interconnectedness, transcendence, and the pursuit of higher inner truths, is a catalyst for cultivating a sense of belonging in resistance. Recognition is in that all beings and elements are connected and that we are a part of a larger web of existence eclipsing individual boundaries, circumstances, and identities. This recognition fosters a sense of belonging. It's the admission that we are not alone in our struggles.

The Healing Power of Collective Practices

With the belief that Earth is not predictable, collective practices rely upon the ability to process complex dynamical systems. As the message or information may not always be easily perceived, it may require an emergence of consciousness to sharpen intuition. The magick is in the enormous opportunity of the fundamentals and manipulation of the unknown. The success of techniques could all be a matter of perspective, interpretation, or expectation. Interpretation is believed to be guided by the ancestors and collective divination supports the conscious processing of messages from spirit.

Healing is an inherent aspect of collective practices rooted in spirituality. In the context of communal healing in the solidarity of resistance, it is also about reclaiming dignity and humanity in the face of oppression. One example of a collective practice is the laying on of hands. As  love is transmitted through touch, our palms can transmit the healing frequencies of love. From pouring a cup of sacred tea to offering sacred fruit or assisting in the cleansing rituals of a member in the community, these are all healing gestures of love.

The laying on of the hands is the transference of intention from one spirit to another. Before partaking in this ritualistic act, there is a prayer or blessing said over the impending touch by opening you up to the laying of the heart onto another in need of healing. Chant, song, or prayer creates vibrational wellness in the communal ritual. Some interpret this as praise or worship;

worship in the context of spirit, not idolization. The laying of hands is considered the first form of energy or divination work. Stemming from the walls inside Kemet temples, there are drawings of Earthly beings giving healing through the palms of their hands and seemingly breathing life force with Maat's feather into the crown of another's head.

Step-By-Step Hands-on Energy Work

1. Cleanse or smudge the work area.
2. Drink a cup of purified water.
3. Conduct a spiritual rinse for yourself and the one who will be receiving the laying on of hands.

   A. Using a small bowl of hyssop water, gently rinse down the face, throat, arms, hands, legs, and feet.

   B. Alternatively, you can use infused Florida water.

4. Next, anoint chakras with. chosen essential oils relative to the purpose of the work.

   A. Frankincense and myrrh are traditionally used.

5. Wash your hands thoroughly with black soap or clay soap with purified water.

  A. Tradition calls for hyssop herbal tea instead of water.

6. Set intentions and call upon the ancestral guides for support and clarity in works. Ask them to send forth healing energies through the palms of your hands.

  A. Only conduct hands-on work upon those who are aware and give permission.

  B. Make sure to center before setting intentions for healing support in hands-on work.

   a. To do this, quiet yourself and visualize yourself in a bubble of divine golden light.

   I. Remember to keep a protective force around your workspace when hosting rituals.

   b. Take a few cleansing breaths and then breathe in deeply seven times, exhaling blockages, confusion, and all doubt that could interfere with the healing flow.

c. As you continue your breathing, focus your awareness on the palms of your hands.

I. Rub them briskly together, before turning your palms toward each other to very gently bring your hands together. You should then feel a bit of resistance in between your hands with this attempt.

7. Now use your palms to feel the energy field with a body scan.

   A. The individual should be lying flat on their back for the scan.

   B. Palms are held about 3 inches above the body, scanning from the top of the head to the bottom of the feet.

   C. Stop when you feel coldness, heat, or something unusual, like a blockage or emptiness.

   D. Take note and continue the scan.

8. Focus your hands on the areas that produce the most heat.

A. Move the energy clockwise with your hands over the spot.

B. Pull up.

C. Push out and draw out the pain or negative energies—each time shaking your hands vigorously to remove energies being discharged.

9. When you feel a release let go of the location—sigh and take a collective cleansing breath.

10. Let the person lay quietly, focusing on their breath, as you do a final scan, envisioning a protective light around them.

11. Let them rise after a minute of deep breathing and gently sit upright in a chair for a few moments with a glass of purified water.

12. Lastly, while this person is sipping water, shake out your hands one more time and wash them in salt water or Florida water.

The intersection of spirituality, resistance, and healing is a powerful byway for transformative healing amongst the members of the community. Group-based interventions are particularly beneficial as they bring communal cultural orientation that heals a sense of detached identity.

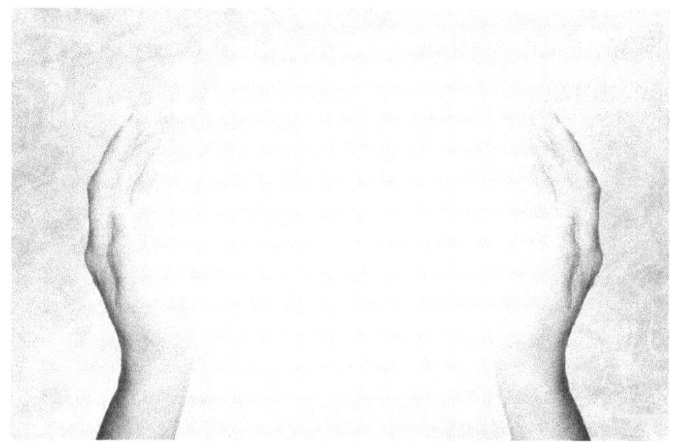

The Community Healing Network and Association of Black Psychologists is an example of a communal program that emphasizes resilience in the communal healing of the African American diaspora. These organizations interact with the community in modern-day healthcare settings. Although they are not direct correlations to the spirituality of ancient wisdom, they are a service for the collective to seek healing or counseling in culturally responsive treatment. They also represent forms of healing functions and important health resources for the community. They serve as restorative functions for the collective to enhance their ethnic experiences and collective freedoms. Either way, the nobility of African American healers affirms humanity in healing the spirit of the African American community. There is an unapologetic sense of comforting liberation when psychological consequence encourages a commitment to others.

CHAPTER 10
LOOKING FORWARD

African American herbalism and magick offer a holistic approach to health and wellness that integrates the physical, emotional, and spiritual realms. As we look to the future, the landscape of African American herbalism and magick is ever-evolving and expansive, presenting both challenges and opportunities for spiritual growth and transformation.

As more of the diaspora rediscover their roots and their ancestral connectivity to the natural elements, a renewed interest in tradition has emerged. However, there is still a lack of access to resources and pertinent historical information that could supplement lore and tradition. African American herbalism isn't just about plant life, strife, and protection from circumstance, but also about lineage and honoring the knowledge of the ancestors. This final chapter will explore the future of African American herbalism and magick by examining the consistent challenges facing practitioners, the opportunities for societal advancement, and the evolving landscape of holistic spiritual practices.

Challenges Facing African American Herbalism and Magick

While African American herbalism and magick face challenges related to systemic inequalities, power imbalances, and cultural appropriation, society has continued to threaten their viability and relevance in history. One of the primary challenges is the ongoing marginalization and erasure of traditional healing practices and overall contributions to Western medicine. Through the intentional manipulation and monopoly of a system, these social inequities remain alive in modern times. It is clear that freedom is first in the free consciousness of the mind.

Despite growing interest in African American herbalism and magick or alternative medicine, the community is underserved, overlooked, and dismissed as lacking substance or capability. This lack of recognition discredits community origins and gives credence to the illegitimacy of ancient Western criticisms of a stolen people. Social evolution is required outside of the proverbial walls of the community in order for the transformation of a people to truly be successful. This evolution should release resources, funding, and opportunities that have been previously unavailable to this marginalized group.

There seems to be a misconception that freedom is controlled by man, when in fact, it is a birthright. Despite the ongoing attempts to erase the history of formerly enslaved people, their traditions, culture, and rituals, a gathering of community counteracts this. The loss of traditional knowledge and practices is attributed to forced assimilation, displacement, and colonization. Forcibly removed from their land of origin and subjected to centuries of cruel exploitation, many families are out of touch with the traditions of generations past. Knowledge has simply been diluted or appropriated. Additionally, pharmaceutical globalization has led to the commodification of indigenous plant knowledge which further erodes the cultural heritage of the African American people. Reawakening the natural capacity to heal oneself is a challenge within itself.

Incorporating celestial knowledge to aid

health disparity has always been labeled as taboo, evil, or dark magic. Misinformed superstition leaves little room for discovery or explanation amongst the mainstream. Limiting access to access to healthcare and safe living environments can be discouraging and keep individuals in a mindset of hopelessness. These structural barriers not only exacerbate transgressions against a people, but also undermine the ability to overcome, heal, and engage in community ceremonies and gatherings.

Opportunities for Growth

From intention to radical hope, the future presents significant opportunities for innovation within the practice of herbalism and  magick. Opportunity lies in the growing disillusionment of Western medicine and the conventional healthcare system. Western medicine, while effective in treating acute conditions, often falls short when it comes to sustaining health and addressing chronic illnesses, mental health issues, or underlying causes of disease. Many people have become disillusioned with the pharmaceutical-driven model of healthcare which tends to focus on suppressing the symptoms, rather than eradicating and addressing the cause.

A key reason for this disillusionment is the overreliance on over-the-counter opioids, pain relievers, and prescription medications, which usually pair with a number of unfavorable side effects and unimaginable risks. As a result, there is a growing interest in natural and holistic alternatives that offer a gentler, more sustainable approach to healing. Often criticized for its lack of focus on preventative care, conventional healthcare also lacks emphasis on lifestyle interventions, neglecting to tend to the importance of diet, exercise, stress management, grief counseling, or other lifestyle factors promoting long-term health and rejuvenation of the mind. There is a growing need for a healthcare approach that embodies the whole person—body, mind, and spirit. As more people seek alternatives to conventional medicine, the opportunity presents itself for the masterful herbalist, spiritual leader, and practitioner to fill the void and meet the needs of the increasingly disillusioned.

The community desires a more personalized and culturally relevant approach to healing.

They need social justice reform to drive the longing for equity. Emphasizing cultural agency, radical hope carries a future of decolonized possibilities. Hope is described as a gift from the ancestors and has survived even the cruelest of slave masters. Hope is evidence of the understanding that there is something greater to achieve than the mundane. It is the physical and mental emancipation from the horrors of historic misfortunes and cultural genocide. Hope is curating new traditions from the remnants of the old as the ancestors were stripped from traditional practices. Situated between the spiritual and socioeconomic context, hope is a symbiotic relationship between community and cultural advancements.

Cultural competency and diversity in the healthcare industry is an opportunity for recognition. As such, there is a growing demand for masterful herbalists or practitioners of alternative medicine who are sensitive to the cultural practices of a diverse community. African American herbalists and spiritual leaders have a leadership opportunity to expand the consciousness of a people exclusively through communal efforts. The future is shaped by determination and innovation. It is important to distinguish cultural competency from individual desires. A commitment to a new collective future for the African American community is just what the doctor ordered to continue to battle injustices.

Although new frameworks are emerging that conceptualize cultural competency, the onset of digital technology and social networking has presented a chance for herbalists to unite the community on a massive scale. Through social media, practitioners and spiritual healers can share the grace of their knowledge with clients and beyond. Virtual consultations are more common than ever now, as opposed to setting up an appointment and entering the presence of spirit through a shared physical space. These online communities build support and solidarity in the culture by keeping traditions relevant and providing access to knowledge. Social media is a space for practitioners to amplify their voices, raising awareness about spiritual levels of the subconscious relative to the divine and advocating for greater recognition and respect for traditional healing practices. By embracing innovation, promoting patient-centered healthcare, and fostering collaboration across disciplines, practitioners of ancient holistic traditions can help to transform and shape the future of healthcare for the African American people.

The Evolving Landscape of Spiritual Practice

Adapting to social changes, cultural and technological landscapes influence the broader field of magickal and spiritual practices. We live in a time where holistic medicine is a viable practice for the mainstream. The growing integration of medical sciences into natural science, traditional healing practices with modern scientific research as well as research and evidence-based medicine have become notable trends. Scientists, researchers, and practitioners join forces to increasingly explore the therapeutic potential of herbal remedies. Seeking to validate the efficacy of plant-based medicine and mind-body practices, rigorous scientific studies and clinical trials are being conducted. Some might say this is done with bias, while others will only believe test and trial results.

There is also a growing concession of the importance of environmental sustainability and ecological stewardship within the field of natural medicine. Deeply rooted, African American herbalism and magick will naturally support action behind the concerns of climate change, environmental degradation, and biodiversity loss. Practitioners are left with the principle to promote not just internal, but ecological balance and natural harmony, such as regenerative agriculture and wildcrafting.

African American herbalism is both promising and challenging. Practitioners must navigate the complex interplay of social, cultural, and environmental factors shaping the art of spiritual medicine, the practice of magick, and the recognition of African American herbalism.

REFERENCES

About sacred botanica bk — sacred botanica. (n.d.). Sacred Botanica. https://www.sacredbotanicabk.com/about-us

Adele, T. (2024, January 12). Healing crystals: Benefits, uses and where to buy. *Forbes Health.* https://www.forbes.com/health/wellness/guide-to-healing-crystals/

Afua, Queen. (2000, April). *Sacred woman: A guide to healing the feminine body, mind, and spirit*

Alabama Cooperative Extension System. (2023, July 18). *Native fruits: Maypop - Alabama cooperative extension system.* https://www.aces.edu/blog/topics/forestry/native-fruits-maypop/

Archives, P. (2009, October 22). *Purple passion flower used as food and medicine.* cherokeephoenix.org. https://www.cherokeephoenix.org/culture/purple-passion-flower-used-as-food-and-medicine/article_76c05564-81d3-548c-8562-fafd18559018.html

Ayales, A. (2017, October 10). THE ENERGETIC PROPERTIES of Passionflower. *Anima Mundi Herbals.* https://animamundiherbals.com/blogs/blog/the-energetic-properties-of-passionflower

Bergner, Paul. (1997). *The healing power of echinacea, goldenseal, and other immune system herbs*

Berry, J. (2023, November 20). *Growing & foraging passionflower & maypops (+ ways to use them!).* Unruly Gardening. https://unrulygardening.com/passionflower-maypops/

Caesar - South Carolina encyclopedia. (2022, July 20). South Carolina Encyclopedia. https://www.scencyclopedia.org/sce/entries/caesa

r/#:~:text=He%20is%20widely%20considered%2
0to,medical%20findings%20appear%20in%20prin
t.&text=Slave%2C%20medical%20practitioner.,for
%20poison%20and%20rattlesnake%20bite.

Coneflowers. (2023, December 4). Almanac.com.
https://www.almanac.com/plant/coneflowers

Deane, G. (2020, November 6). *Maypops mania - eat
the weeds and other things, too*. Eat the Weeds and
Other Things, Too.
https://www.eattheweeds.com/maypops-food-
fun-medicine-2/

Divination | Religion, history & practices. (2024,
February 2). Encyclopedia Britannica.
https://www.britannica.com/topic/divination/Var
ieties-of-divination

*Divination and spirit possession in the Americas |
Encyclopedia.com*. (n.d.).
https://www.encyclopedia.com/history/encyclope
dias-almanacs-transcripts-and-maps/divination-
and-spirit-possession-americas

Dr. Sebi - BrandMentions Wiki. (n.d.).
https://brandmentions.com/wiki/Dr._Sebi

Dr. Sebi's Cell Food. (n.d.). *Method*. Dr. Sebi's Cell
Food. https://drsebiscellfood.com/pages/method

Founders of Urban Moonshine. (2016). *DIY Bitters: A
guide to making your own bitters*

From Africa to America. (n.d.). The Pluralism Project.
https://pluralism.org/from-africa-to-america

Gardiner, B. (2024, January 7). The magic of mugwort,
the mother of herbs - the outdoor apothecary. *The
Outdoor Apothecary*.
https://www.outdoorapothecary.com/mugwort/

Georgia Native Plant Society. (2020, December 11).
Sassafras (Sassafras albidum) - GNPS. GNPS.
https://gnps.org/plant/sassafras-sassafras-
albidum/

Herbal bitters. (n.d.). The Herb Society of America -
South Texas Unit. http://www.herbsociety-

stu.org/herbal-bitters.html

Horehound | Joel Lane museum house. (n.d.). https://www.joellane.org/history/the-gardens/horehound

Horehound - Marrubium vulgare. (n.d.). Monticello. https://www.monticello.org/house-gardens/in-bloom-at-monticello-3/horehound/

Horehound — Northern Arizona invasive plants. (n.d.). Northern Arizona Invasive Plants. https://nazinvasiveplants.org/horehound

How to make salves, ointments and balms. (2012a, October 5). Whispering Earth. https://whisperingearth.co.uk/2011/06/19/how-to-make-salves-ointments-and-balms/

Johnstone, G. (2022, April 11). *How to grow and care for mugwort (Artemisia vulgaris).* The Spruce. https://www.thespruce.com/how-to-grow-mugwort-5077403#toc-how-to-care-for-mugwort

Joiner-Siedlak, M. (2022, April 5). *Throwing the bones - Monique Joiner Siedlak.* Monique Joiner Siedlak. https://mojosiedlak.com/throwing-the-bones/

Josh. (2018, August 13). *Ancient passion flower benefits.* Healthy Hildegard. https://www.healthyhildegard.com/passion-flower-benefits/

LAc, M. D. D., & LAc, M. D. D. (2022, December 13). *Herbs for protection: the science and spirit of sage and mugwort.* CHOQ®. https://choq.com/herbs-for-protection-the-science-and-spirit-of-sage-and-mugwort/

Little medicine thing: Emma Dupree, herbalist - ECU Digital Collections. (n.d.). https://digital.lib.ecu.edu/58575

M. Griggs, M. (n.d.). *Sassafras albidum (Nutt.) Nees.* https://www.srs.fs.usda.gov/pubs/misc/ag_654/volume_2/sassafras/albidum.htm

Maypop-passion flower – passiflora incarnata | Root Buyer. (n.d.). https://rootbuyer.com/maypop-passion-flower-passiflora-incarnatea/

medicinal herbs: maypops - passiflora incarnata.
(n.d.).
https://www.naturalmedicinalherbs.net/herbs/p/
passiflora-incarnata=maypops.php

Medicinal practices of enslaved peoples. (n.d.-a). The
College of Physicians of Philadelphia.
https://collegeofphysicians.org/programs/educati
on-blog/medicinal-practices-enslaved-peoples

O'Driscoll, D. (2022, April 24). Sacred Tree Profile:
Sassafras' Medicine, magic, mythology and
Meaning - The Druids Garden. *The Druids Garden
- Spiritual journeys in tending the living earth,
permaculture, and nature-inspired arts.*
https://thedruidsgarden.com/2017/08/20/sacred-
tree-profile-sassafras-medicine-magic-mythology-
and-meaning/

Osuch, B. (2022, September 1). *How to grow, harvest
and preserve echinacea.* Seed to Pantry School.
https://seedtopantryschool.com/grow-harvest-
preserve-echinacea/

Passion Flower. (2020, June 18). HerbaZest.
https://www.herbazest.com/herbs/passion-
flower#medicinal-properties

Phelps, Latham M. (2012, January). *The Family of
Henrietta Phelps Lawson Jeffries of Halifax
County Virginia and Caswell County, North
Carolina*

Rd, A. P. M. (2020, June 18). *Goldenseal: benefits,
dosage, side effects, and more.* Healthline.
https://www.healthline.com/health/goldenseal-
cure-for-everything

Religion and slavery | slavery and remembrance.
(n.d.).
https://slaveryandremembrance.org/articles/articl
e/?id=A0059

Ross, W. (2022, January 21). *Throwing the bones:
Finding your future.* Spirituality+Health.

https://www.spiritualityhealth.com/articles/2021/02/05/throwing-the-bones

Singh, C., & Bhagwan, R. (2020). African spirituality: Unearthing beliefs and practices for the helping professions. *Social Work/Maatskaplike Werk, 56*(4). https://doi.org/10.15270/56-4-882

Spirituals | ritual and worship | musical styles | articles and essays | the library of congress celebrates the songs of America| digital collections | library of congress. (n.d.). The Library of Congress. https://www.loc.gov/collections/songs-of-america/articles-and-essays/musical-styles/ritual-and-worship/spirituals/

Take back your uterus with this psychedelic Herbof the ancient world |. (n.d.). https://sites.evergreen.edu/plantchemeco/mugwort/

The Editors of Encyclopaedia Britannica. (1998, July 20). *Cairn | Ancient, prehistoric, monument.* Encyclopedia Britannica. https://www.britannica.com/topic/cairn

The influential Black herbalists who inspire practitioners today - Brooklyn Botanic Garden. (n.d.). Brooklyn Botanic Garden. https://www.bbg.org/article/black_herbalists_harriet_tubman_emma_dupree#:~:text=Doctor%20Caesar%2C%20an%20enslaved%20man,narrowleaf%20plantain%20and%20common%20horehound.

United Plant Savers. (2022, January 21). Goldenseal cultivation & growing guide. - united plant savers. *United Plant Savers.* https://unitedplantsavers.org/goldenseal-cultivation-growing-guide/

United Plant Savers. (2023, July 21). *Goldenseal – hydrastis canadensis - united plant savers.* https://unitedplantsavers.org/species-at-risk-list/goldenseal-hydrastis-canadensis-2/

VanDyke, Lucretia. (n.d). *African American herbalism: A practical guide to healing plants and folk traditions.*

Van 'T Klooster, C. I. E. A., Haabo, V., Ruysschaert, S., Vossen, T., & Van Andel, T. (2018). Herbal bathing: an analysis of variation in plant use among Saramaccan and Aucan Maroons in Suriname. *Journal of Ethnobiology and Ethnomedicine, 14*(1). https://doi.org/10.1186/s13002-018-0216-9

Xules, L., & Xules, L. (2023, September 17). *The many roles of a master herbalist.* Xula Herbs. https://www.xulaherbs.com/blogs/blog/the-many-roles-of-a-master-herbalist

CLICK HERE

Or Visit Below:

https://www.subscribepage.com/svmyth

Simply scan the qr code to join.